FENCES, WALLS, AND HEDGES FOR PRIVACY AND SECURITY

Fences, Walls, and Hedges for Privacy and Security

Jack Kramer

DRAWINGS BY ADRIAN MARTINEZ
(unless otherwise noted)

CHARLES SCRIBNER'S SONS
New York, N.Y.

Contents

Introduction: Fences and the Landscape Plan

With land at a premium and house sites small, just how you fence your garden and property is almost as important as the house you choose. Our little Edens are indeed vital to our well being and so is our privacy and security in what is becoming a very crowded world. However, walls do not a prison make if the walls—fences, screens, and hedges—are planned with thought for the total landscape.

Wood fences, glass and plastic screens, and concrete or brick walls are some ways to both beautify and ensure our privacy. These structures should and can add to the property rather than detract from it. With today's new materials there are dozens of fence and wall designs to build and most of them are do-it-yourself projects. What you ultimately choose in the way of a fence depends on the individual site and your personal tastes and we offer many suggestions in this book to help you find the best fence for your situation. The main point is that the fence or wall should be part of the total landscape plan and not a tacked-on afterthought. Or, as a matter of fact, an insult to your neighbor (who wants his property to look lovely too).

Natural "fences" of trees or shrubs are another possibility especially in urban areas where noise, as well as air pollution, is a problem. Trees and shrubs can screen out noise by ten decibels, or almost fifty percent, as well as help to thwart pollutants in the air.

So whether in city or country, in small house or large home, fences are a prime consideration of landscaping. In this book we tell you about dozens of fences and walls, and show you how to build them to assure and ensure your private green world.

JACK KRAMER

*FENCES, WALLS, AND HEDGES
FOR PRIVACY AND SECURITY*

1. Property Boundaries

Years ago fences or property boundaries were really unnecessary because there was plenty of land, and generally the lot next to you was empty. Not so today—the world is indeed becoming small, and good building sites are difficult to find. So where once defined boundaries were not needed, today if the homeowner wants a modicum of privacy and security, fencing, screening, or some barrier, man-made or natural, is desirable.

The fence or screen may provide privacy or protection from the weather, or help reduce noise. Fencing also defines your property and can (and should) be a handsome addition to the site, fitting into the setting rather than looking like a tacked-on afterthought. A fence is as much a part of the landscape plan as the plants and trees within it. Remember too that in most cases the fence will be visible and you will see it, so it should be decorative and functional, not just a barren expanse of wood or concrete.

Once a fence was made only of wood, but today there are many materials to use: brick, concrete blocks, stone, glass, and so forth. Thus the design of the fence no longer has to be a straight line of boards.

Shapes and Sizes

The shape and size of the site is a determining factor in choosing a fence and deciding what it should be made from. The architecture of the house itself is equally important; for example, some homes need a rustic wood fence, contemporary houses look best perhaps with a concrete decorative block wall, and traditional homes usually need masonry or wooden boundary lines.

Lots can be rectangular, pie shaped, wedge shaped, or square. Each shape will influence what kind of fence to build. Again, your house and the general character of the neighborhood will dictate the fence design and materials to use—stone, wood, glass, concrete, or plastic.

Let us consider the rectangular site. If you simply fence it, it will look like a box and be more liable to imprison you than be a pleasing addition. A stepback fence, a shadowbox pattern, or any other distinctive design will alter the monotony of a rectangle. The fence may

This simple but elegant wood fence defines the property; it separates the house and garden from the natural background. It is never obtrusive but rather seems to bring a cohesive effect to the total setting. (*Photo by Ken Molino*).

Screening out an ugly view, this high wooden fence uses a diagonal design to make it attractive. While it is a barrier it is a pleasant one to look at. (*Photo courtesy California Redwood Assoc.*)

frame some of the property (it usually does) or in some cases, for example, where street noises are a consideration, enclose all the property. Consider all these factors before building.

Square lots, like rectangular ones, are somewhat difficult to fence because a box-like design is hardly interesting. Try to use a patterned rather than a straight fence; the latter might make the property seem smaller than it is.

If the lot is wedge or pie shaped, you have more liberty for fence layout. You can have the fencing repeat the lines of the site, always a pleasing plan, or try some curved fencing to soften the strong lines of a triangular lot.

A masonry wall is used for privacy as well as for its charm. Though heavy in appearance the pattern of stonework is appealing. (*Photo by Matthew Barr*)

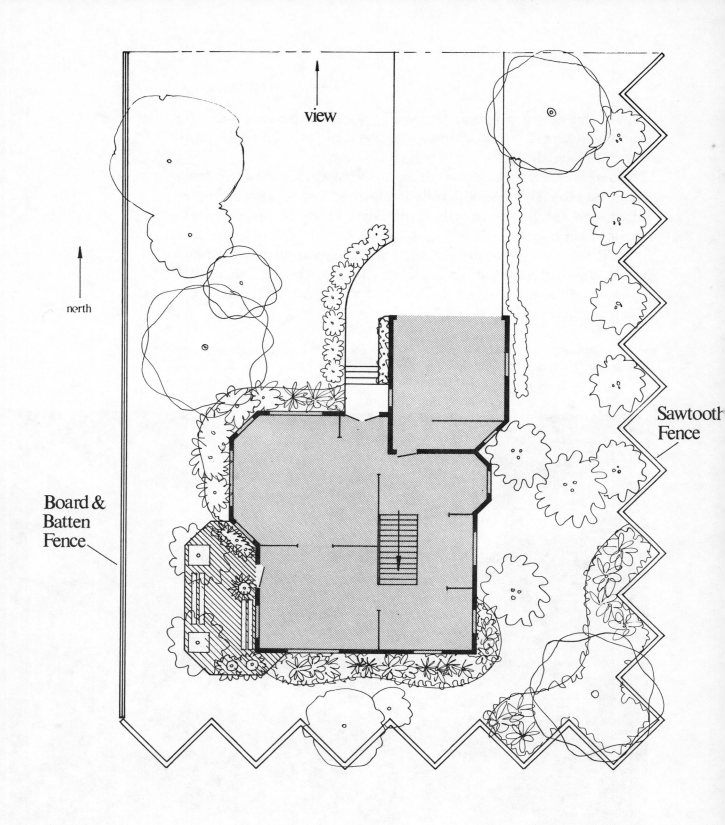

view

north

Board &
Batten
Fence

Sawtooth
Fence

Fence for Rectangular Site

With any lot, if there is a handsome view, take advantage of it (do not screen it out); use glass, a combination of glass and wood, or a grid design so you can see out. On the other hand, if there is an eyesore, by all means screen it out completely. But do not construct a straight blank wooden wall; use a board-and-batten fence or perhaps a louvered design.

A fence is not simply a fence, so work out designs well ahead of time on paper before you build. Remember that once a fence is in place it is costly to dismantle.

PRIVACY AND SECURITY

As mentioned, years ago privacy and security were less important, but today these factors are as important as the choice of the house. Our homes are our sanctuaries, and privacy is of vast importance in our scheme of living. After a day in a crowded city we want some seclusion, a place to relax. The trouble with privacy is that if we screen out all vistas, we end up in a total prison, so the design of a fence must be carefully executed.

Security too is a major factor these days, and a good fence goes a long way in discouraging unwelcome guests such as burglars. You do not want a fortress, yet you want something substantial that will please the eye and at the same time provide some measure of protection from intruders.

A concrete or wooden fence is ideal for privacy and security. However, if the site is suitable, and there is appropriate landscaping, a strong hedge of laurel or boxwood can also serve as an effective barrier. The advantage is that this kind of green fence blends well with landscaping and is a welcome relief from more substantial wooden or stone barriers. A hedge screening will be equally formidable, and intruders will think twice before scaling such a "wall."

Fretwork fences or grid designs offer beauty and still allow light and air to enter the property. These fences do not give complete privacy, but they generally make it difficult for anyone on the outside to see through.

WEATHER AND NOISE CONTROL

Few people realize that fences also help to temper weather conditions; placed properly, a fence can thwart strong winds. Try to determine the way the wind strikes your yard before selecting a fence style. It may seem that a solid board fence is the best protection from wind, but this is not true. A solid fence stops the wind on one side, and then it flows over the fence to flow down to ground level on the other side. But a slatted or louvered fence will thwart the wind because the slats or laths diffuse it.

This decorative fence actually separates the property itself and is used more as a dividing screen to create a patio area. (*Photo by Ken Molino*)
A handsome wooden fence shuts out the street; the fence itself is decorative and functional. Spaces between the vertical members allow light and air to enter so plants can grow. (*Photo courtesy California Redwood Assoc.*)
This slat fence of horizontal and vertical design is handsome and architectural, almost an extension of the house. Redwood planters complement the setting. (*Photo courtesy California Redwood Assoc.*)

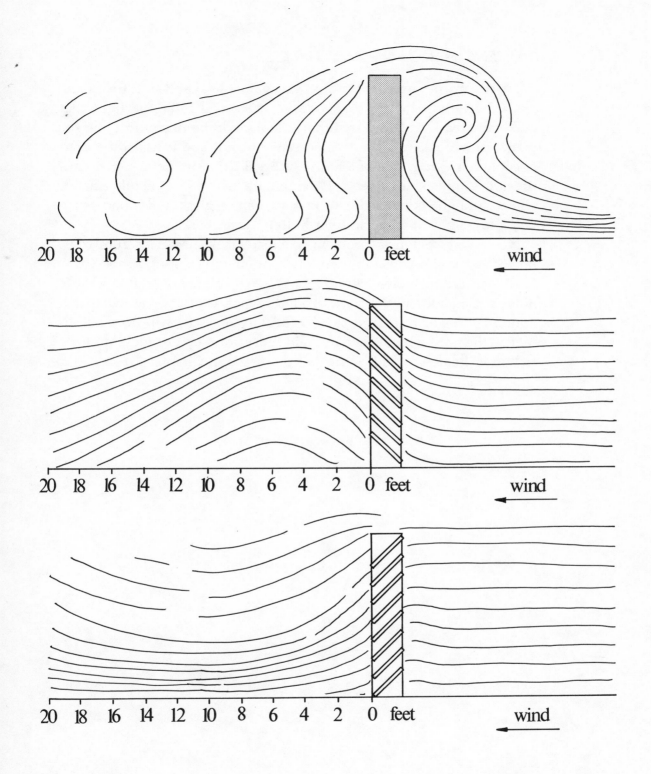

20 18 16 14 12 10 8 6 4 2 0 feet

wind

20 18 16 14 12 10 8 6 4 2 0 feet

wind

20 18 16 14 12 10 8 6 4 2 0 feet

wind

Wind Currents

Fences are also excellent protection against heat and sun; for example, a louvered, slot, or basketweave fence will filter the light and make an area livable, where otherwise it could be uncomfortable for plants or people. A fence that screens out hot sun can also be used to cool the western side of a house; it breaks the sun before it reaches the house and so heat does not accumulate inside. On the other hand, where sunlight is needed, say in a garden, a glass and wood fence will allow light to enter and yet buffet strong winds.

Noise was seldom a problem in most areas, urban or rural, but now it is a major consideration when buying or renting property. A fence can reduce noise levels from street or highway traffic. Traffic noise can be quite bothersome around homes, especially at peak rush hours. Fences of trees and shrubs (heavily massed) will do much to reduce the noise level, whereas solid fences of wood or glass do little to buffet the noise. (This is further discussed in Chapter 7.)

2. Fence Facts

Once you have decided what kind of fence you need and for what (weather protection, privacy, and so on), you need to determine just where it should go. But before you start designing the layout you must know something about the legal aspects of fences; for example, local building codes dictate fence construction as to height and placement in relation to setbacks from streets. Also of prime importance are your neighbors and their property, or fences built between adjoining landowners. Many times a survey is necessary to determine where a fence can be located.

Only after you have decided on the kind of fence and have checked building codes is it time to actually lay out the fence. And this is best done on paper so you can rectify any errors easily before constructing.

Local Building Laws

Local building codes vary greatly from state to state. In some locales there are restrictions against using a high fence to enclose a front yard. The legal reasons are varied but essentially make good sense, so do check first with local authorities. Some areas may have a restriction against wire fences of hazardous natures—barbed-wire and electrical fences, in particular, and the use of glass fences also carries restrictions in many states. In addition, in some places the planning office may require that you erect a fence; this is especially true for swimming pools in California; these areas must have fences to prevent accidents and mishaps. So once again, checking with the local building-codes department, the community planning office (if there

9

is one), or city and county offices is the way to determine what is and is not allowed. It is not simply a case of this is my property and I'll do with it what I want. The people who control building codes have done extensive studies, and their information is invaluable to you; there are valid reasons behind all regulations. Many towns, especially in the Northeast, require a building permit for putting up a fence. The cost is nominal.

A fence built *between* two property owners is generally considered as belonging to whomever owns the land on which it is built. But a *line* or *division fence* belongs jointly to the neighboring property owners as tenants in common. In either situation you may be able to get your neighbor to agree to share expenses on a fence, or if he is not interested in this arrangement, he may give you written consent to put up a fence. This simple piece of paper can prevent distressing situations later if disputes do arise. The easiest way to approach the problem is to consult with your neighbor before you build.

Fence Layout

At first glance laying out a fence may seem simple: Put stakes in the ground and start building. Don't do it! First have a plot plan. They may be obtained from the title insurer's survey for the bank putting out the mortgage; sometimes you can get a plan from your contractor, if a new house, or occasionally from a former owner, if an old house. Study the plan to determine exposures and how sun strikes the property. With the plot plan as a guide, make a rough

Local building codes regarding fences vary in states; generally a 6-foot fence is maximum. This decorative wood fence is a good-neighbor fence, equally handsome from both sides. (*Photo courtesy California Redwood Assoc.*)

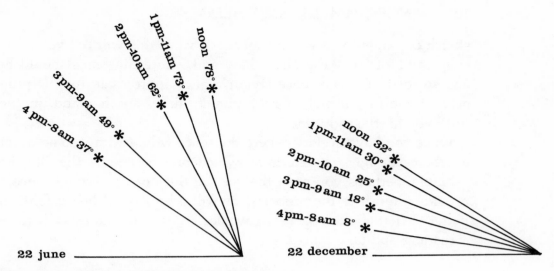

2pm-10am 62°
1pm-11am 73°
noon 78°
3pm-9am 49°
4pm-8am 37°

noon 32°
1pm-11am 30°
2pm-10am 25°
3pm-9am 18°
4pm-8am 8°

22 june

22 december

SUMMER and WINTER SUN ANGLES latitude 34°

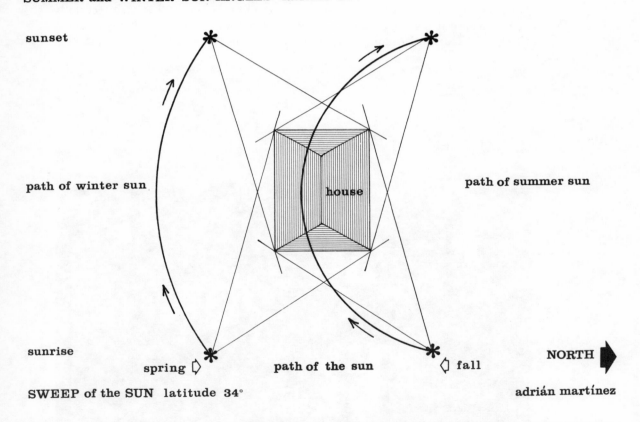

sunset

path of winter sun

house

path of summer sun

sunrise

spring ◊

path of the sun

◊ fall

NORTH ▶

SWEEP of the SUN latitude 34°

adrián martínez

The Sun & Orientation

sketch on paper. You will be surprised what this will tell you about shape and site of the ground, how and where the fence should be, and so forth. Draw a fence layout that is appropriate for the property; if the first sketch is not suitable, draw another and another until you hit the right one.

Once you have decided where the fence will be, draw some different fence designs to determine which one best suits the site. For example, perhaps you need the vertical lines of a louvered fence to provide interest to the property, or will a horizontal board fence be better? What about a basketweave design or, if the house calls for it, a rustic grapestake fence?

Note the layout of this fence; it is never straight or boxy, and is architecturally right because it just skirts the slope area—a natural definition (*Photo courtesy California Redwood Assoc.*) (*Photo by Ken Molino*)

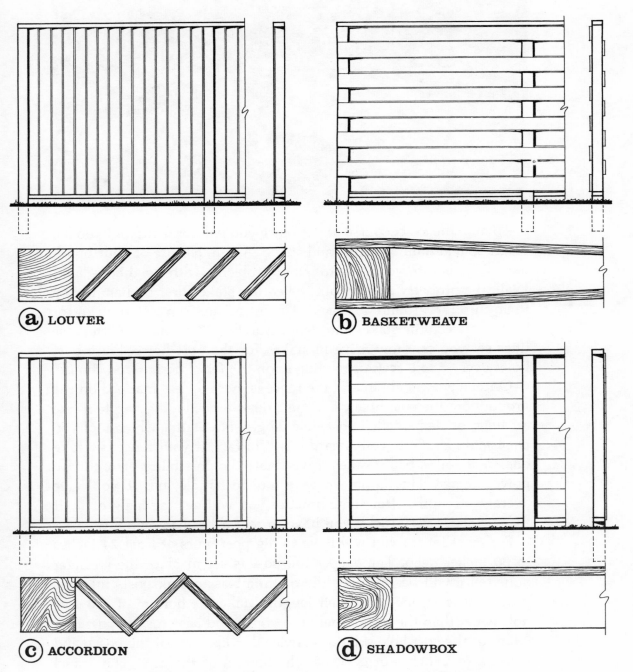

a LOUVER

b BASKETWEAVE

c ACCORDION

d SHADOWBOX

note: posts - 4x4's   rails - 2x4's   boards - 1x6's   all redwood

Types of Fences

To map the exact course of the fence you will need stakes (wooden pieces sold at lumber yards) and string. Again, be sure of your boundary lines before you start to avoid problems with neighbors later. Walk the property and lay out the corner stakes first by hammering them into the ground at specified points. Then run nylon string or twine between the stakes and tie it securely to the stakes. With these lines set you can now drive in stakes for the post holes. Place post holes every 6 to 8 feet, depending upon the fence design you choose.

Once all stakes are in and the fence is more or less mapped on the ground, dig the post holes. For this you will need a digging tool like an auger or clam-shelled post-hole digger. No matter which tool you choose, digging into soil is hard work. In fact, if your fence is a long one, or if soil is badly caked, investigate the possibility of renting a power digger. This is not an easy tool to handle, but if you have average strength, after some practice you will get the hang of it. If the surface is very rocky you have to rent a jackhammer.

For most fences you will have to dig post holes at least 24 inches to 30 inches deep. The deeper the post is set in place the stronger your fence will be. A good rule of thumb is to sink posts into the ground at least one-third their length. Make the bottom of the post hole wider than the top so there is a good solid base for the post (the width of the post hole should be twice the diameter of the post), and insert 2 to 4 inches of gravel at the bottom of the hole. The gravel will eliminate any water that accumulates at the bottom, which can cause wood to rot.

To set the post in place (this is called plumbing the post), shovel some gravel into the hole and put the post on top of it. Add several

14

This painted fence is exceedingly decorative and fits the architecture of the home. A large-scale or natural wood fence might have been out of place. (*Photo by Ken Molino*)

① **MARK FENCE LINE WITH STRING GUIDE**

② **SET POSTS IN CONCRETE OR DIRECTLY IN GROUND**

③ **ALIGN POSTS BETWEEN CORNERS WITH STRING**

④ **NAIL RAILS AT TOP & BOTTOM**

⑤ **INFILL WITH DESIRED DESIGN & MATERIALS – MISC. SHOWN**

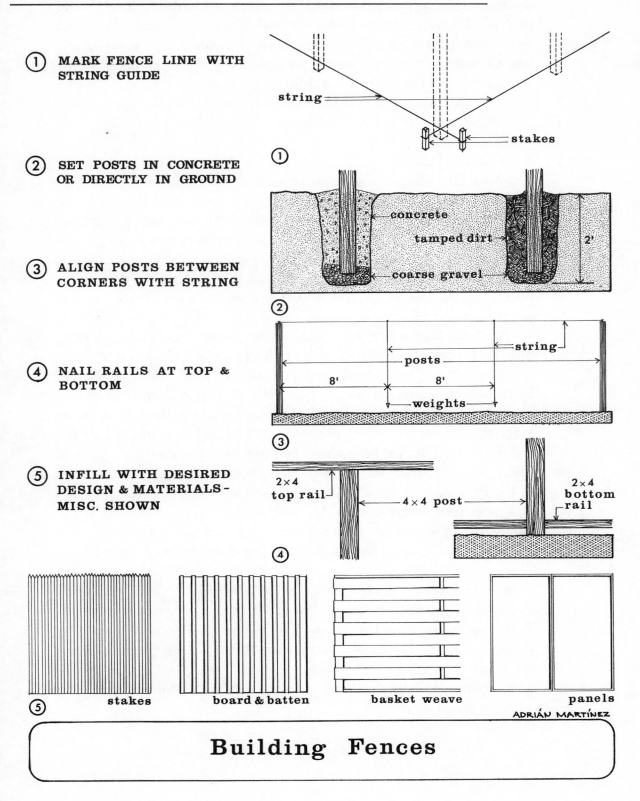

① string — stakes

② concrete — tamped dirt — coarse gravel — 2'

② posts — string — 8' — 8' — weights

③ 2×4 top rail — 4×4 post — 2×4 bottom rail

④ stakes — board & batten — basket weave — panels

⑤

ADRIÁN MARTÍNEZ

Building Fences

shovelfuls of concrete, juggle the post slightly, and then check the two sides with a carpenter's level. Add the concrete so it is flush with the ground, and then again check the two sides with the level. If the post is not correct, move it slightly and correct the alignment. Use a lean concrete mix: 1 part cement, 3 parts sand, and 6 parts gravel (see Chapter 6). The mix should be rather dry, never runny. Once it is aligned, hold the post by hand for a few minutes. It takes about 15 minutes for concrete to harden, and I do not nail on stringers (horizontal timbers) for at least 36 hours.

BUILDING THE FENCE

The actual building of the fence varies with the design used and who builds it. I put all posts in place, attach stringers, and then nail the vertical members in place. For a simple fence this is a good procedure.

Another method is to assemble the fence in sections—fitting in the rails and pickets whenever two line posts are in place. In other words, the sections are built on the ground and then fitted into place. The problem with this procedure is that the sections are heavy, so two people instead of one are necessary.

Attaching the stringers or rails and the vertical members (pickets, boards, grapestakes, and so on) to the posts is the easiest part of fence building. There is only one precaution: Stringers or rails must be firmly and squarely attached to posts or you will have problems later. The lap joint is the simplest one to use to attach rails to posts. Place the rail on top or against the post and nail it in place. I prefer the butt joint: Hold rails against the posts and toenail them in place. This is stronger than the lap joint because the posts support the ends of the rails by friction. The perfectionist uses the mortised joint, but this takes time and considerable know-how. A rectangular hole is cut partly or all the way through the post, and then the rail is eased into the cut. This creates a very solid fence but does take experience.

Attaching Pickets, Boards, and Other Members. Once the posts and rails are up the vertical members are ready to be nailed in place. This is easy to do but takes time. The main consideration is that the spacing must be absolutely perfect (uniform). Cut a piece of wood the exact dimension of the space you want, and use this as a guide when nailing pickets or boards in place. Do not skimp on nails; use

There was no need for a tall fence here and yet some dividing line between the garden and the forest was necessary. A simple brick wall was used, adding charm to the area. (*Photo by Matthew Barr*)

enough to really hold the vertical members in place solidly; they should not touch the soil. Allow at least 2 inches clearance.

Preservatives.   Redwood and cedar can be used without any preservatives and will last a long time. However, some protection is necessary, especially where any wood member touches the ground or on surfaces like joints where moisture can collect.

Wood preservatives, available at hardware dealers, will protect your fence for a long time. There are two kinds: water borne and oil borne. Water-borne preservatives contain salt, so it is best not to use them in the garden because salts are poisonous to plants and, being soluble in water, can leach out into the ground. Creosote is an oil-borne preventative and a good one. It is long lasting and insoluble in water. However, creosote is generally used only on members sunk into the ground. Do not paint creosote on the bottom of posts; rather, if possible, dip them into the creosote so the wood can soak up the preservative.

Other good preventatives for wood are the pentachlorophenol forms. They come in a variety of trade names and make wood almost completely resistant to water penetration; for example, Penta, which is water repellent and ideal because you can paint over it.

Wood preservatives can severely injure skin, so take care when handling them and try not to get any on your hands. Wear gloves and carefully follow directions on the can.

A good-quality paint will also protect wood fencing, but it has no protective value under ground, and if there are any cracks or splits in the wood, decay spores can get in under the paint and cause havoc. Thus paint cannot be considered a complete preservative, although it does have its uses and you can certainly use it. But be especially careful of the color you select: Be sure it relates to rather than clashes with the garden. White is a traditional color for fences, but the earth colors (browns, siennas) are also desirable. For best results, use a base coat and then, after it dries, one or two coats of outdoor paint. It is much simpler to paint all pieces before they are assembled, but often this takes considerable work (bending and squatting). I find it easier to paint the fence when it is up and then touch up hammer marks and nailheads. Your paint store dealer can advise you about types of fence paint.

PROBLEM AREAS

If a tree is in the way in the line of a fence, there are ways to solve the dilemma. It is ridiculous to remove a handsome tree because of a fence. Instead, stop the fence a few inches from the trunk, and then start the fence again on the other side by cantilevering the two sections of the fence that butt to the tree. The cantilever construction allows you to place the fence posts a distance from the tree; thus you will not injure the root system when you dig the post hole.

This fence is built at angles to conform to the property; it is simple wood construction and does the job well. (*Photo by Matthew Barr*).

If you have a simple wooden fence, a tree in the way can be saved by incorporating it into the fence; simply cut a contour in the fence to accommodate the tree. Under no circumstances should you use the tree as a joining member for a fence because nailing into the tree can rip open bark and allow disease or fungus to enter the tree.

If your land is hilly, fence construction will be rough but not impossible. For steep slopes simply follow the contour of the land, laying out the fence design in steps. Step-type fences look handsome because of their pattern. Simply canting a fence to fit a hillside is another method, but this is very difficult, and lining up posts and rails so they are exact and precise requires professional help.

Design Help

If your property is large or you do not have time to lay out your own fence, and you have a landscape architect planning your garden, consult him on fence design too. He can give you a finished drawing of the fence, or if you want only advice, you can pay him by the hour. Or of course you can go it alone. But after building several fences for my own homes, I now work in conjunction with a landscape man, who I hire by the hour for his advice and rough sketch. Then I contract for the labor and material. I have post holes dug (tough work) and the posts set in concrete. I do the final nailing of the fence myself.

If the cost of consulting a professional is beyond your budget, often your city building inspector or county agent can give you excellent helpful suggestions free. Distributors of prefabricated fences will also provide free information on how to put up their fence, and wood associations offer an array of helpful catalogs on how to design your own fence and how to build it! You can write these associations for booklets:

California Redwood Association
617 Montgomery Street
San Francisco, California 94111

Western Wood Products Association
1500 Yeon Building
Portland, Oregon 97204

Hiring a Fence Company

Having someone do the job for you after you have supplied the design of the fence you want saves much time and labor. But it is not cheap. The prices I have had from most fence contractors were extremely high, but remember that if you go this route, the fence goes up quickly, and you do not lift a finger. If you hire professional help, have a written contract made, specifying the grade of lumber to be used, types of preservatives for wood posts, how deep the posts are to be sunk, whether posts are to be in concrete or soil, and so forth. Everything should be spelled out so there is no problem later when work is in progress. Written agreements are worth their weight in gold; verbal agreements are often forgotten.

3. Lumber Facts

Lumber, a versatile building material, is usually sawed, drilled, and nailed with little trouble. But how to use the right kind of lumber (there are many grades, just as there are grades in meats or in clothing) is rarely discussed. Also, most people do not understand how to buy lumber; for example, when you buy a 2 x 4 foot piece of lumber you do not get a 2 x 4. Rather, the actual dimensions are 1 9/16 x 3 9/16.

Redwood is generally the best lumber for fence construction because natural chemicals within it serve as protection against termites and fungus. It can be used without a protective coating and will weather beautifully to a silvery color, or it can be stained or painted according to your tastes. Preservatives should be used on underground portions of posts. Redwood is easy to work with, has fine grain, and, perhaps most importantly, blends well with outdoor surroundings.

Cedar is another good durable wood; however, it is difficult to find and costly. It too weathers well and needs little protection against the elements. On the other hand, Douglas fir, less expensive than redwood or cedar, has a tendency to rot when exposed to severe weather conditions. If you must use it, be sure to give it protective coatings, as mentioned in Chapter 2.

GRADES
Lumber comes in grades. Generally your lumber dealer will advise you as to what you need for your fence, but I always believe in

knowing something about what I am buying, not only to get my money's worth, but to work better with the material I am using. Here is how lumber is graded:

Clear Heart Redwood. A superior (and expensive) all-heartwood grade for architectural use. Highly decay-resistant and free of knots. Can be used for posts.

Select Heart. All-heartwood grade that has some small knots and torn grain. High strength and durability.

Construction Heart. A good commercial decay-resistant grade with some large knots.

A-Grade. May contain cream-colored sapwood. Is less resistant to decay than all-heartwood grades. Free of imperfections.

Construction Common (rough lumber). Similar to Construction Heart except that sapwood and medium stain are permitted and it has tight knots.

Merchantable. Contains more knots and defects (loose knots and knotholes in some areas) than the higher sapwood grades. Economical for fence boards.

Kiln-dried lumber (more expensive) is not required for fences, although it is sometimes used for posts or ornamental members; air-seasoned lumber generally performs fine. However, lumber that is too green (has too much moisture) is likely to shrink and pull loose from fastenings after a time.

The various grades of lumber have many surface textures. Clear Heartwood, A-Grade, and Common Grade generally are surfaced on both sides to a smooth finish. Select Heart or Construction Heart may come from the mill with a rough surface. It is satisfactory for fencing members but difficult to paint. Saw-textured lumber is not the same as rough lumber; it is more expensive and has a handsome resawed quality.

Even within the specific grades of lumber there are variations, so it is a good idea to personally select your lumber rather than having it selected for you. You can select boards with less defects. Also I have found frequently that lumber will be warped or not square.

Garden grade lumbers.

This is allowable in the lumber trade but can wreak havoc for the amateur carpenter.

Most fences are built with 4 x 4 posts, 2 x 4 rails or stringers, and 1-inch boards. For top and bottom rails of fences and posts use an all-heartwood grade of lumber. For fences taller than 6 feet use 4 x 6 or 6 x 6 posts. Rails for heavier structures may call for 2 x 4 lumber. For posts and other near-ground structural members use Construction Heart; natural chemicals in the wood protect it from decay and termite attack. Lumber with sapwood (Construction Common, A-Grade, for example) can be used for board members and where wood is well off the ground.

> Vertical members are 1 x 2 Construction Heart redwood; the slightly curving fence admits cool breezes while partially obscuring yard from outside. (*Photo courtesy California Redwood Assoc.*)

Here 1 x 4 redwood boards are used; the designer specified Construction Grade redwood because of economy and also because of the informality imparted by the knots. (*Photo courtesy California Redwood Assoc.*)

DIMENSIONS OF LUMBER

As mentioned earlier, the actual size of a piece of wood is not what the dimensions say, so for easy reference here is a table of standard dimensions (in feet):

Kiln-dried Lumber

Size to Order	Actual Size (measured in inches)
1 x 4	3/4 x 3 1/2
1 x 6	3/4 x 5 1/2
1 x 8	3/4 x 7 1/4
2 x 4	1 1/2 x 3 1/2
2 x 6	1 1/2 x 5 1/2
2 x 8	1 1/2 x 7 1/4

Unseasoned Boards
(generally used for fencing)

Size to Order	Actual Size (all measurements in inches)
1 x 3	25/32 x 2 9/16
1 x 4	25/32 x 3 9/16
1 x 6	25/32 x 5 5/8
1 x 8	25/32 x 7 1/4
2 x 3	1 9/16 x 2 9/16
2 x 4	1 9/16 x 3 9/16
2 x 6	1 9/16 x 5 5/8
2 x 8	1 9/16 x 7 1/2
2 x 10	1 9/16 x 9 1/2

DETERMINING HOW MUCH LUMBER FOR FENCING

Stock-sized lumber is based and priced on even-inch dimensions; for example, a 2 x 4 board comes in 8-, 10-, or 12-foot lengths. Bear this in mind when ordering.

Trying to determine how much lumber you need for a specific property fence can be complicated if you have to convert from lineal to board feet. But this is not necessary; all lumber dealers will help you with this facet of fence building. Tell them how much running feet of fence you need and how tall you want it, and they will send you the right amount of stringers, posts, and vertical members, all cut to size. This, of course, will be more expensive than cutting the lumber yourself, that is, ordering 1 x 6 boards 12 feet long and cutting them 6 feet high, or whatever. The cost of having them cut is higher than if you cut them yourself because of the extra labor involved. So if you have a good power saw, buy lumber and do the cutting yourself. If you do not have a saw, you will simply have to pay the price.

By the way, lumber is delivered tail gate, that is, dumped in one specific spot; then it is up to you to move it to the fence site. Thus you should tell the deliveryman *exactly* where you want the lumber: Get it dumped as close as possible to the fence site to save you from carrying it around.

A simple board fence, easy to build and so handsome; framed openings are used to add flair to the design. (*Photo courtesy California Redwood Assoc.*)

Hardware

Lately there has been an increasing use of hardware—L brackets (corner braces), T clamps, and so forth as ornamental motifs on fences. These attractive hardware appointments will add beauty to the fence as well as help in its construction. The combination of, say, black galvanized-iron designs against redwood is a handsome look and can do much to make a bare fence attractive.

Also useful on fences are metal or black wrought-iron pot holders and brackets to accommodate container plants. Use a row of these along a wall or stagger them for an equally effective picture. This arrangement, especially for large expanses of fence, will greatly diminish the blandness of an uninteresting wooden fencing.

27

Construction Common Redwood is used for this step-down fence in author's garden; here the choice was of economy because there was so much fencing needed. (*Photo by Matthew Barr*)

Nails and Fastenings

Non-corrosive nails and fastenings should be used outdoors. Recommended nails are made of stainless steel or aluminum alloy. Top quality, hot-dipped galvanized nails will also perform well if the galvanized coating is not damaged during nailing. The slight additional cost of non-corrosive nails is justified by their superior performance.

Do not use plain iron, steel, or cement-coated nails, or nails galvanized by other than the hot-dip process. Contact with moisture will corrode these fastenings, form black discolorations on the wood surface, and cause nails and screws to lose their holding power.

4. Wood Fences

Today's fences are both beautiful and functional and, as explained in Chapter 1, can be used in many different designs in many different ways. But basically the fence made of wood is the most popular one. Whether you choose a lattice, board-and-batten, panel, or picket fence (becoming very popular now), it should complement the house and garden.

Kinds

Fences can be classed as picket, rail, split rail, post and rail, post and board, lapped joint, grapestake, slat, louver, board, basketweave and lattice. This sounds like many, and it is; let us look at each type and see what it can or can not do for your property so selection can be made simple.

The picket fence is lightweight in appearance, and the openness of the structure does not present a fortress look. Picket fences are trim and simple and add elegance to a property. Generally they are painted white, and the repetitive quality is what gives the fence its design. The tops of the pickets may be triangular, saw toothed, angled, rounded, arrow shaped, and so forth. Pickets may be decorated with acorns or pyramids, pineapples, or a flat cap at post intervals to add interest to the fence. The fence may even be arched or bowed by using different picket heights.

The picket fence is fine as a low barrier, say 3 or 4 feet tall, but it does not provide complete privacy or very much protection from the wind. It is more decorative than functional, but for the Colonial house or variations of it, a picket fence makes a handsome addition.

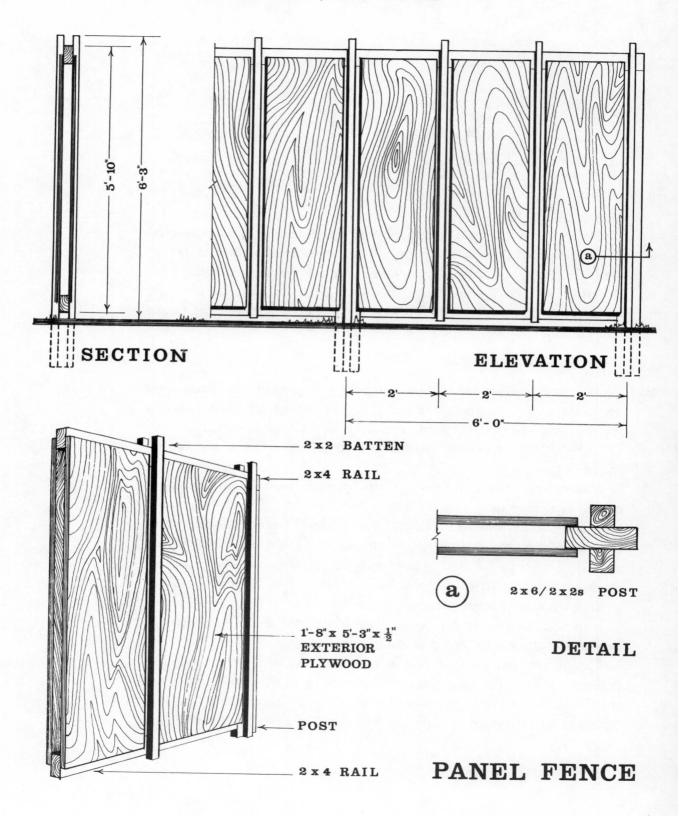

SECTION

ELEVATION

2'   2'   2'

6'- 0"

2 x 2 BATTEN

2 x 4 RAIL

a   2 x 6 / 2 x 2s POST

DETAIL

1'-8"x 5'-3"x ½"
EXTERIOR
PLYWOOD

POST

2 x 4 RAIL   PANEL FENCE

Picket fences are charming and used frequently; they are one of the easiest fences to build and are generally painted white. (*Photo by Matthew Barr*)

Patterns of sunlight and shade add a changing dimension to this latticework fence; a really handsome effect. (*Photo courtesy California Redwood Assoc.*)

This rustic stake fence is very handsome next to the pool and it affords complete privacy. (*Garden design by Eleanor B. McClure, photo by Roche*)

A straight board fence, easy to build and yet quite attractive; note shadowbox effect used to break the expanse of wood. (*Photo by Ken Molino*)

Pickets are built with standard-sized boards such as 1 x 2, 1 x 3, or 1 x 4.

The rail fence is fine for the country scene, where privacy is no factor and the horizontal design fits well into rolling or flat terrain. It is generally economical and easy to build, but it is not decorative or good for privacy. This is a real pioneer fence which evolved when wood was plentiful and boundary lines were flexible. These fences require only casual workmanship and may be in a zig-zag design or split rail. Post and rail design is sometimes seen too. Basically, the rail fence is not a good solution for today's properties.

Slat fences are simple to build, contribute greatly to a site, and look handsome in almost any situation. Material generally used is rough-finished redwood sawed into 1 x 1-inch or 1 x 2-inch strips. The design is somewhat formal but always neat, and these fences can provide complete privacy. Tests indicate that an open slat fence provides very effective wind control, with closely spaced slats breaking up and dispersing the wind. Slats can be run vertically close together or spaced apart; they may also be used horizontally for a different look or even in combination with vertical slats for a dramatic effect. In the simplest application slats are nailed over post and stringer frame. All in all, a slat fence is a good usable barrier, easy to build and always pleasing.

If you need a windbreak and still want a good-looking fence, consider the louver design. By fixing the louvers accordingly you can still have maximum light, and shade too. And when faced across the path of prevailing winds a louver fence will temper the wind but still allow air circulation.

Vertical-spaced louvers give some privacy but part of the garden will always be visible through the fence as a person moves along it. For complete privacy, use the horizontal design. The louver fence has a strong architectural look and should be carefully matched to the design of the house itself. Buildings with simple square clean lines seem to be in keeping with the louver design.

With louver fences you will need a larger amount of material than with any other wooden fence. Also, because the louvers are supported only at the ends, warping and twisting might occur; thus, many times expensive kiln dried lumber is used. This is a heavy fence too, and

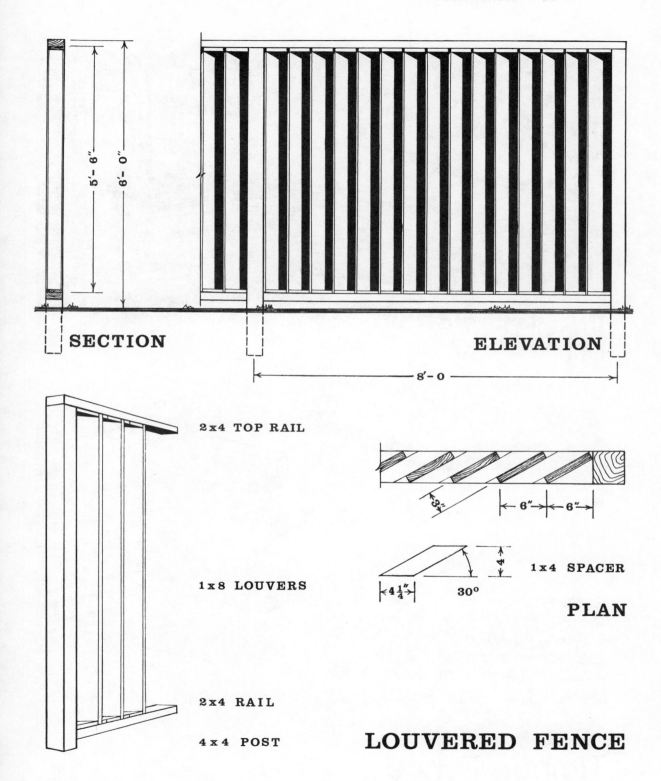

SECTION

ELEVATION

5'- 6"

6'- 0"

8'- 0

2x4 TOP RAIL

3½"

6"   6"

1x8 LOUVERS

4"

1x4 SPACER

4 ¼"   30°

PLAN

2x4 RAIL

4x4 POST   **LOUVERED FENCE**

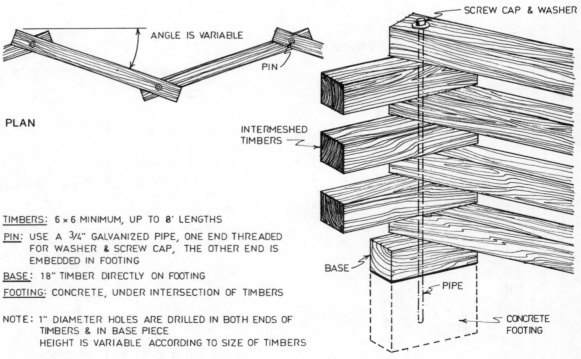

ANGLE IS VARIABLE

PIN

PLAN

SCREW CAP & WASHER

INTERMESHED
TIMBERS

BASE

PIPE

CONCRETE
FOOTING

TIMBERS: 6 × 6 MINIMUM, UP TO 8' LENGTHS

PIN: USE A 3/4" GALVANIZED PIPE, ONE END THREADED
FOR WASHER & SCREW CAP, THE OTHER END IS
EMBEDDED IN FOOTING

BASE: 18" TIMBER DIRECTLY ON FOOTING

FOOTING: CONCRETE, UNDER INTERSECTION OF TIMBERS

NOTE: 1" DIAMETER HOLES ARE DRILLED IN BOTH ENDS OF
TIMBERS & IN BASE PIECE
HEIGHT IS VARIABLE ACCORDING TO SIZE OF TIMBERS

Timber Fence

drawing: Adrian Martinez

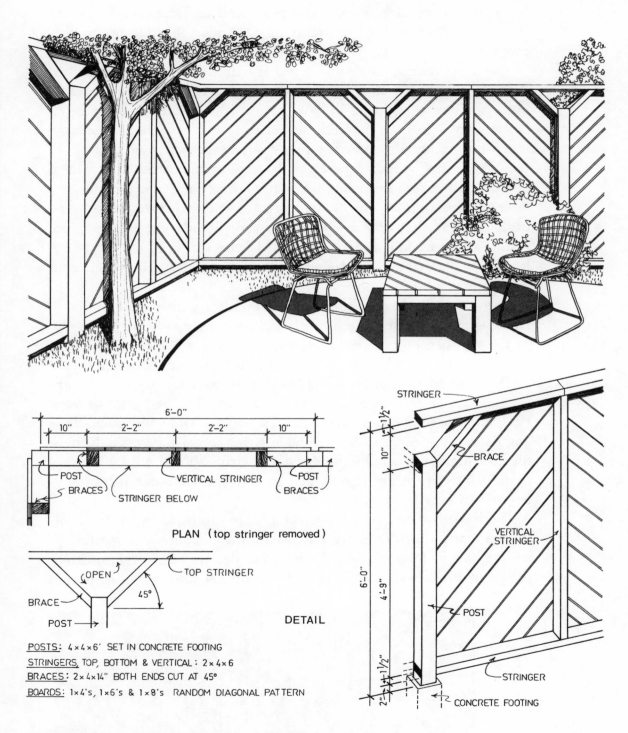

PLAN (top stringer removed)

POST
BRACES
VERTICAL STRINGER
STRINGER BELOW
POST
BRACES

OPEN
BRACE
45°
POST
TOP STRINGER

DETAIL

6'-0"
10"   2'-2"   2'-2"   10"

STRINGER
1½"
10"
BRACE
6'-0"
4'-9"
VERTICAL STRINGER
POST
1½"
2"
STRINGER
CONCRETE FOOTING

POSTS: 4×4×6' SET IN CONCRETE FOOTING
STRINGERS, TOP, BOTTOM & VERTICAL: 2×4×6
BRACES: 2×4×14" BOTH ENDS CUT AT 45°
BOARDS: 1×4's, 1×6's & 1×8's RANDOM DIAGONAL PATTERN

Diagonal Board Fence

design/drawing: Adrian Martinez

the structure requires substantial posts and foundations. Yet even with its problems a louver fence is a handsome addition to the property.

The designs and variations of board fences are limitless, and this is a simple fence to build. The solid design provides maximum privacy but often creates a boxed-in look, so use it only for small areas. A better idea is to space boards, say ½ to 1 inch apart, or if privacy is a prime factor, instead of setting boards together leave space and then cover the vertical spaces with 1 x 1-inch boards to create a design. Boards placed slantwise within the frame also provide an interesting variation. Thin batten designs, either horizontal or vertical, in somewhat of a trellis effect, can provide eye interest and result in a handsome design. The board fence can fit into almost any landscape plan (the exact design will depend on the house itself and the boundary lines).

Board fences are generally easy to build; a sturdy post and rail frame is made and the boards are attached in easy fashion. Use 6 x 6 or 4 x 4 posts set 6 to 8 feet apart and 2 x 4s can serve as rails. These fences are heavy so be sure to use substantial foundations for them.

The attractive appearance that the basketweave fence gives on both sides makes it quite popular. The design may be horizontal or vertical, and the weave can vary from flat to very wide and open. Triangular designs made of thin wooden strips can also be used. Rough finished lumber is usually preferred and strips should not be thinner than ½ inch or thicker than 1 inch. A favorite width is 6 inches and length can vary from 14 to 18 feet.

The basketweave fence looks complicated to build but actually it is not; many times rails are not used and it is simply a matter of nailing strips at posts. Cost is minimum, dealers offer prefabricated panels of basketweave fencing and all you need do is nail to posts.

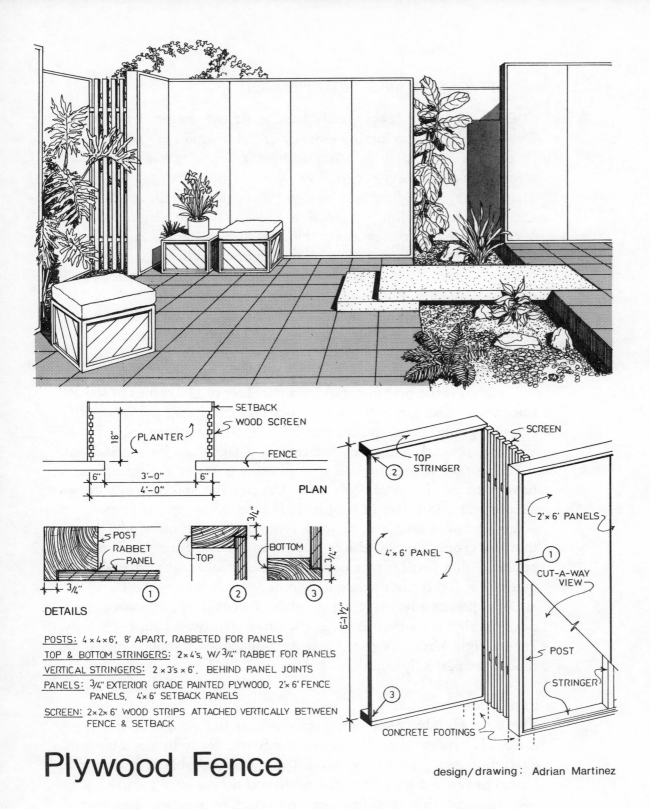

PLAN

SETBACK
WOOD SCREEN
18"
PLANTER
FENCE
6"   3'-0"   6"
4'-0"

DETAILS

POST
RABBET
PANEL
3/4"
①

3/4"
TOP
②

BOTTOM
3/4"
③

SCREEN
TOP STRINGER
②
4'×6' PANEL
2'×6' PANELS
①
CUT-A-WAY VIEW
POST
6'-1½"
③
STRINGER
CONCRETE FOOTINGS

POSTS: 4×4×6', 8' APART, RABBETED FOR PANELS

TOP & BOTTOM STRINGERS: 2×4's, W/ 3/4" RABBET FOR PANELS

VERTICAL STRINGERS: 2×3's×6', BEHIND PANEL JOINTS

PANELS: 3/4" EXTERIOR GRADE PAINTED PLYWOOD, 2'×6' FENCE PANELS, 4'×6' SETBACK PANELS

SCREEN: 2×2×6' WOOD STRIPS ATTACHED VERTICALLY BETWEEN FENCE & SETBACK

Plywood Fence

design/drawing: Adrian Martinez

More a divider than a fence, this structure is sculptural and yet functional. The places for plants is an especially fine idea. (*Photo courtesy California Redwood Assoc.*)

Trellis or lattice fences really have more use than at first glance. Depending upon the lumber—heavy or light—and the grilles—close together or far apart—the fence provides many versatile designs and always looks handsome. A tightly woven lattice fence can give complete privacy; a slightly open design allows air to circulate. All in all, the trellis fence is quite adaptable and imparts an elegant, almost Victorian feeling to a property. However, these fences are not easy to construct and require painstaking attention to detail.

Panel fences made of hardwood pressed board or more popularly of plywood offer several advantages: The fence goes up quickly, there is a wide range of materials to use, and panels give complete privacy. You will need strong structural support for this fence and it is wise not to use it in very long expanses because it will be confining.

Plywood is the best material for a panel fence and comes in several thicknesses and sizes; the 4 x 8-foot size the best; always specify exterior grade. Panel fences can be decorated with wood grids or shadowbox work and many interesting designs can be worked out.

Grapestake fences are still seen in some parts of the country and have a rustic charm of their own. Usually the stakes are 2 inches square and 3 to 6 feet in length. This kind of fencing is favored by some because it is so easy to work with. Stakes can merely be driven into the ground or nailed like pickets to a fence frame and may be applied either vertically or horizontally, or in alternating panels. The material is lightweight, easy to handle, and decay-resistant. Yet for all its apparent advantages, grapestake fences to my eye always appear shabby and never as elegant or neat as sawed boards or slats. For the right kind of house, where a rustic look is wanted, grapestake fences are perfectly suitable.

PREFABRICATED FENCES

The term prefabricated simply means that the design of the fence is already predetermined; you buy the fences ready to assemble with all components. There are several designs available (for example, basketweave and post or rail), and if you do not care to make your own designs, this is a fine way of selecting fencing. Remember, though, that when you buy a prefabricated kit fence generally you do not get the posts with it; that is a separate cost.

A wood batten fence has simple clean lines and is unobtrusive in the garden.
(*Photo by Roger Scharmer*)
A step-down board-and-batten fence can be attractive and is easy to build; it
affords privacy. (*Photo by Matthew Barr*)

A wooden rail fence painted white defines this property and is a fine foil for
plants. (*Photo courtesy California Redwood Assoc.*)

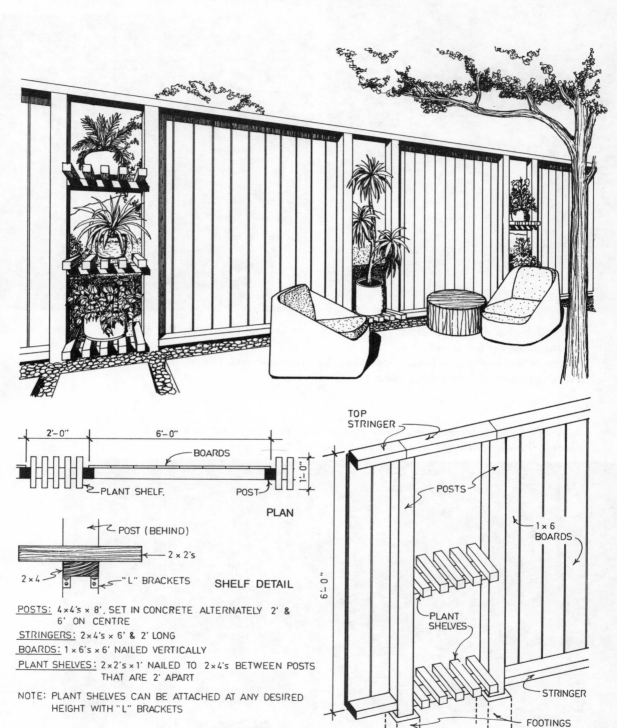

2'-0"   6'-0"

BOARDS

PLANT SHELF.   POST   1'-0"

PLAN

POST (BEHIND)

2 × 2's

2 × 4   "L" BRACKETS   **SHELF DETAIL**

TOP STRINGER

POSTS

1 × 6 BOARDS

6'-0"

PLANT SHELVES

STRINGER

FOOTINGS

POSTS: 4 × 4's × 8', SET IN CONCRETE ALTERNATELY 2' & 6' ON CENTRE

STRINGERS: 2 × 4's × 6' & 2' LONG

BOARDS: 1 × 6's × 6' NAILED VERTICALLY

PLANT SHELVES: 2 × 2's × 1' NAILED TO 2 × 4's BETWEEN POSTS THAT ARE 2' APART

NOTE: PLANT SHELVES CAN BE ATTACHED AT ANY DESIRED HEIGHT WITH "L" BRACKETS

Plant Shelf Fence

design/drawing : Adrian Martinez

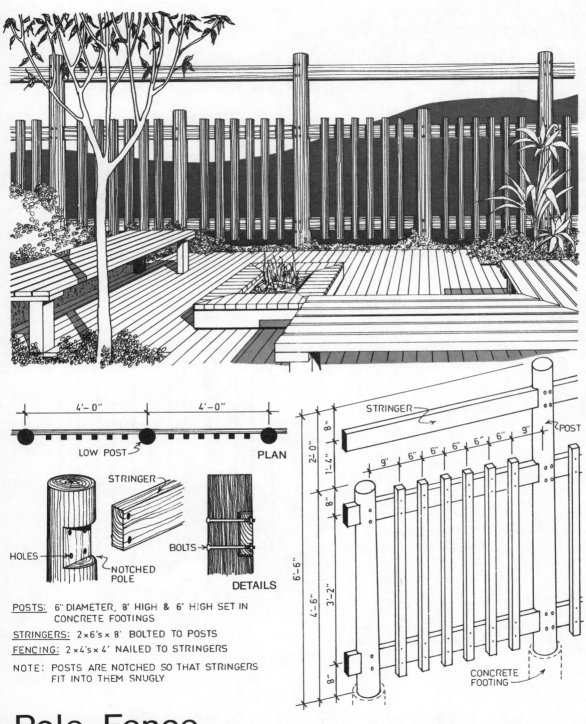

LOW POST

PLAN

STRINGER

HOLES

STRINGER

NOTCHED POLE

BOLTS

DETAILS

POST

STRINGER

CONCRETE FOOTING

POSTS: 6" DIAMETER, 8' HIGH & 6' HIGH SET IN CONCRETE FOOTINGS

STRINGERS: 2×6's × 8' BOLTED TO POSTS

FENCING: 2×4's × 4' NAILED TO STRINGERS

NOTE: POSTS ARE NOTCHED SO THAT STRINGERS FIT INTO THEM SNUGLY

Pole Fence

drawing: Adrian Martinez

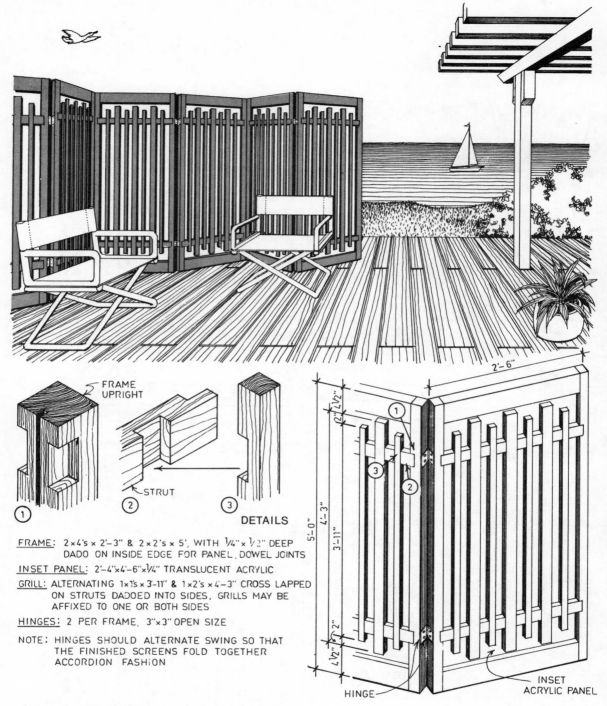

DETAILS

FRAME UPRIGHT

① ② STRUT ③

FRAME: 2×4's × 2'-3" & 2×2's × 5', WITH ¼" × ½" DEEP
   DADO ON INSIDE EDGE FOR PANEL, DOWEL JOINTS

INSET PANEL: 2'-4"×4'-6"×¼" TRANSLUCENT ACRYLIC

GRILL: ALTERNATING 1×1's × 3'-11" & 1×2's × 4'-3" CROSS LAPPED
   ON STRUTS DADOED INTO SIDES, GRILLS MAY BE
   AFFIXED TO ONE OR BOTH SIDES

HINGES: 2 PER FRAME, 3"×3" OPEN SIZE

NOTE: HINGES SHOULD ALTERNATE SWING SO THAT
   THE FINISHED SCREENS FOLD TOGETHER
   ACCORDION FASHION

2'-6"

2"   4½"
5'-0"   4'-3"   3'-11"
4½"   2"
HINGE

INSET
ACRYLIC PANEL

Moveable Screen

design/drawing: Adrian Martinez

Simple wooden fences like this add great appeal to today's home; construction
is easy. (*Photo by Roche*)

PLANTER FENCES

Generally we think of fences as straight lines in one dimension, to be planted later, perhaps with vines. However, the place for plants (planters) can be incorporated into the design of the fence for a very effective picture.

Openings in the fence, somewhat like frames on a wall, can also be built into a fence and thus provide a place for hanging plants. Framed openings may be narrow or wide, depending upon the size of plant you intend to use. Aesthetically, three openings in a row are more attractive than, say, one single opening by itself. Step fences are still another way of creating a distinctive fencing and also incorporating planters.

OTHER FENCE DESIGNS

Pole fences patterned after Japanese designed structures are another possibility and provide a handsome look. They are open more than most fences but have a simple elegance that is suitable for many properties. Here, the posts are round rather than square and this lends a somewhat different look that is quite appealing.

The paneled plywood fence with space for planters is another popular design. Where panels are placed one next to another it is wise to incorporate small screen areas, as shown in the drawing, to break the monotony of the wood expanse.

Still another idea is a movable screen fence, and while these are not easy to build they offer privacy when you want it or can be removed at will so you can enjoy a view. These portable screen fences come in handy for many problem sites.

5. Glass, Plastic, Wire, and Iron Fencing

Wood is probably the most popular fencing material, but other materials such as glass and plastic, aluminum and wire also have their uses as barriers. Glass or plastic in combination with wood offer the homeowner a latitude in designs, and glass especially is desirable for shutting out wind while maintaining a view. Also, glass or plastic allows light to enter a garden, definite advantage for growing plants. However, these materials have disadvantages: Glass is expensive, hard to handle, and must be installed with great care; plastic is cheaper than glass or wood, easy to work with and light weight, but it does fade with time.

Aluminum panels have recently been used with some success as fencing, although this material seems out of place in the usual landscape. Wire fences, certainly not decorative, are excellent security barriers and ideal for confining pets or children. In combination with wood, wire fences can be decorative, so do not immediately dismiss this kind of fence. Years ago wire fences were less expensive than wood, but when I built my recent house I was surprised to find wire fencing more expensive than wood. But where security is of prime consideration, wire is an excellent choice.

GLASS FENCES

The glass fence is excellent for keeping wind from the property and yet maintaining a view or for allowing sunshine and yet providing a boundary. In most cases glass gives a sophisticated look to a property and blends well with wood or brick for a very ornamental design. There are many glass patterns available: Some offer complete privacy, and others allow only shadows to be seen on the other side.

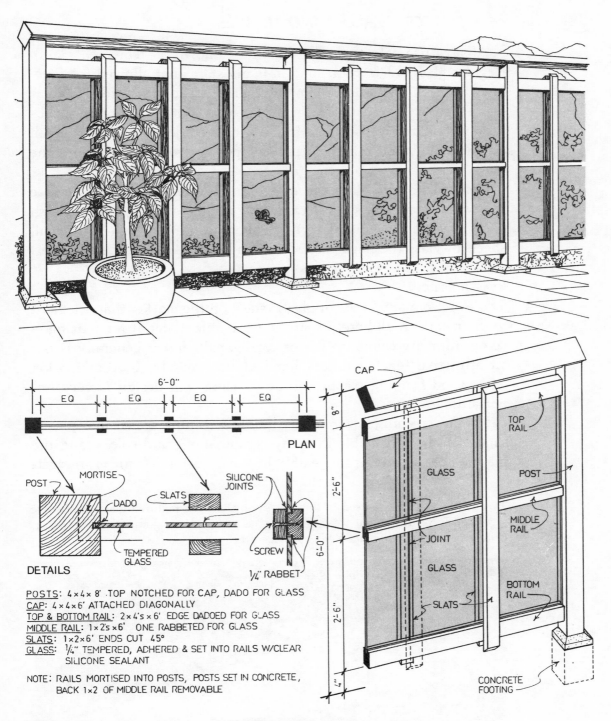

PLAN

6'-0"

EQ   EQ   EQ   EQ

DETAILS

POST

MORTISE

DADO

TEMPERED GLASS

SLATS

SILICONE JOINTS

SCREW

1/4" RABBET

CAP

8"

2'-6"

6'-0"

2'-6"

4"

TOP RAIL

GLASS

POST

MIDDLE RAIL

JOINT

GLASS

BOTTOM RAIL

SLATS

CONCRETE FOOTING

<u>POSTS</u>: 4×4×8' TOP NOTCHED FOR CAP, DADO FOR GLASS
<u>CAP</u>: 4×4×6' ATTACHED DIAGONALLY
<u>TOP & BOTTOM RAIL</u>: 2×4's×6' EDGE DADOED FOR GLASS
<u>MIDDLE RAIL</u>: 1×2's×6' ONE RABBETED FOR GLASS
<u>SLATS</u>: 1×2×6' ENDS CUT 45°
<u>GLASS</u>: 1/4" TEMPERED, ADHERED & SET INTO RAILS W/CLEAR
      SILICONE SEALANT

NOTE: RAILS MORTISED INTO POSTS, POSTS SET IN CONCRETE,
      BACK 1×2 OF MIDDLE RAIL REMOVABLE

Glass & Wood Screen

design/drawing : Adrian Martinez

Always use safety glass (sometimes known as tempered glass). Regular glass is hazardous and in many states not allowed for fencing. But even when using tempered glass, avoid large areas of clear glass that can be mistaken for an opening. Put furniture or shrubbery in front of it, use some brightly colored decals on it, or install a handsome wood railing to prevent people from walking into the glass areas.

Construction of glass fences requires professional help because the wooden members must carry the weight of the glass (¼-inch glass in large sheets is heavy). It is best to use a design with small sheets of glass (perhaps framed in wood) rather than large expanses.

PLASTIC FENCING

There are so many kinds of plastic sheet on the market that it is hard to discuss them all here. Plastic is a versatile material for fencing—comes in many colors, in flat or corrugated—but it generally is not an attractive fencing unless handled very wisely. In combination with wood framing plastic can be pleasing, but design is very important.

Plastic screening is common window screening sealed in a plastic sandwich. It is available in many combinations and colors, and the material has a variable range of light transmission. Plastic is an excel-

Two kinds of glass are used in this fence; on the right textured glass to obscure view and in center a heat-treated clear glass to cut down glare from the water. (*Photo courtesy California Redwood Assoc.*)

This lovely garden uses corrugated plastic panels as fencing; they are framed in painted wood moldings. (*Roehrs display garden, photo by Roche*).

lent choice used to reduce wind velocity and light transmission. Furthermore it is cheaper than glass or wood and very easy to work with. The average person can put a plastic fence together (installed with molding strips or battens) with little trouble at minimum cost. However, in the long run it can be troublesome because generally after a year or so the plastic-screening panels crack or craze and need replacement.

Plastic panels (fiberglass) are available in flat or corrugated sheets in many colors and patterns. This may seem an ideal fencing material, but, even though it is impervious to weather conditions, after some time it appears grimy and faded if in sun. Also, it never really looks at home in a garden and does not blend well with plants; there is always something artificial about it. Yet plastic paneling is cheap, easy to install, an effective wind break, and allows diffused light to enter the garden (excellent light for plants).

Other advantages are that plastic sheets are lightweight, easy to handle, can be sawed or cut even by the novice, and a fence goes up rapidly, generally in one afternoon, and it is the cheapest fencing material you can buy. The corrugated sheets were first on the market, but they are ugly. The flat sheets are more pleasing to the eye and in combination with wood can be handsome; for example, white plastic panels contrast handsomely with dark wood framing. So do use plastic if you want it, but design the fence carefully.

ALUMINUM PANELS

Aluminum-panel fencing is relatively new. Design varies greatly, from board on board to basketweave to simple solid panels enclosed in wood. As a fencing material it is certainly satisfactory because it offers permanence, strength, and low maintenance. Its problem is that it is not indigenous to a garden setting, but in small properties aluminum does have a pleasing look. It is available in many colors and finishes but is not easy to work with because it is somewhat heavy and difficult to put together.

The panels are installed with either aluminum or wood posts. Fencing is available in different heights: 3 to 4 feet or 5 to 6 feet.

Look long and hard at aluminum panel fencing before you go that route. As mentioned, for small properties it can be suitable, but where a natural look is wanted it is out of place. Generally, aluminum fencing must be installed by a professional.

WIRE FENCING

You may balk at the idea of a wire fence around your home because it has connotations of prisons and commercial buildings, but when in the right place and when built properly wire fences can be satisfactory. And wire is your best material for security. The trick with wire is to combine it with other materials such as wood; wire can become an attractive fencing with proper framing and wood grids. A common application of wire is wire mesh attached to wooden posts; sometimes rails are added for appearance. The wire mesh comes in many patterns—hexagonal, triangular, square—and many weights. What you choose depends upon the design and degree of security you need.

The all-wire fence generally comes as a complete unit with posts, rails, mesh, and gates. There are several patterns, usually designated as chain-link or as metal-picket types. The latter is usually made

---

Flat rigid plastic has many applications; here it is used with wood to create a handsome fence. (*Photo by Ken Molino*)

With an Oriental motif, this fence is white rigid plastic with wooden members; it is simple and elegant. (*Photo by Ken Molino*)

Wire fencing need not be unattractive; here it is used in a simple wooden frame and is handsome. The fence offers a safety barrier and still allows you to see the garden below. (*Photo by Ken Molino*)

of plain or plastic-coated galvanized steel. The chain-link fence is galvanized steel, aluminum coated, or plastic coated in a wide range of colors. Green is the most acceptable and blends in more readily with plants than other colors.

The wire fence requires an expert to install, so do not tackle it yourself. It is a difficult job—the bracing and anchoring of corner posts, the stretching of wire, and the general handling of the large rolls of wire are extremely hard to manage.

ORNAMENTAL IRON FENCES

Iron fences have a splendor and beauty that are distinct but however beautiful they are, they are also costly. Some are very ornate, others a simple picket design, and where a dramatic note is needed, iron fences are most effective. If you are considering such a fence have a professional install it. Working with iron is difficult and requires professional know-how.

Manufacturers of iron fencing can show you a wide variety of designs or will make your design to any specification. Some of the old iron fences are intricate and beautifully designed and occasionally appear at salvage shops. Such fencing blends well with contemporary or traditional houses but because of cost large expanses would be prohibitive. Still, where there is a small area to fence, ornamental ironwork can be a worthwhile investment.

An ornamental iron fence is perfect for this small garden; it is complemented with tall hedges beyond to make a stellar statement. (*Photo by Hedrich Blessing*)

6. Walls

The terms walls and fences may seem synonymous, but they are not; because a wall can do many things a fence cannot. For example, walls can be used within a garden to define an area, such as a low wall at the edge of a flower border. But walls can also define a property in the same way a fence does. Yet by their very nature—stone, brick, cement—walls impart still another character to a size. A 6-foot brick wall substantially deadens sound or acts as protection against hot sun. In addition, walls—especially brick and stone— have an old-time quality that is charming in a garden.

You can tackle small decorative walls for breaking the property (up to 3 feet) by yourself. Higher walls will require foundations. This means digging and pouring concrete that is not beyond the average person, but high solid-concrete walls should be done by professionals. Making wood forms and pouring great amounts of concrete can be tricky for the novice.

Check local building codes about walls, heights, and frost lines (how deep you have to dig to install a solid foundation so freezing will not crack the wall), and also check to see if a building permit is necessary.

KINDS

There are as many designs for walls as there are for wooden fences. Brick is the most popular material, but concrete and decorative blocks, cement, and stone are other good materials. Design will of course vary with the material, and each wall will give the property a different look. The brick wall is perennially charming and well

52

Decorative concrete blocks make handsome walls; here two patterns are combined to make an appealing setting of texture and dimension. (*Photo courtesy National Concrete Masonry Assoc.*)

This block wall is simple and attractive; it is not difficult to build and is reasonable in cost. (*Photo by Matthew Barr*)

suited to large property but too heavy for small sites. The concrete-block wall (in the right design) fits almost any situation, as do decorative blocks. Stone walls are infinitely handsome and provide a rustic look; they are fine for most properties (but not all).

The easiest walls to build are those of concrete or decorative blocks. This is a comparatively rapid procedure, and the average handy person can do it.

Concrete and Decorative Block.   For walls, block is the most exciting and versatile of building materials. There are blocks with color (green or tan) cast in them, or you can paint them with rubber-based masonry paints or use them in their natural grey color by water-proofing them with a silicone liquid. There are patterned and textured blocks that can be used in a great variety of designs—stacked, staggered, running bond, on end. There are ordinary aggregate heavy blocks, but for walls you will want to use the lightweight kind because they give better insulation, more effectively deaden sound, and are easy to lift. The most common size is 16 inches long, 8 inches high, and 8 inches wide. Foot-square and 4-inch blocks are on the market, and blocks are also available in brick shapes, except they are solid rather than hollow. In addition to the standard block there are half, corner, double-corner, bullnose, and channel blocks to help you make wall building easy.

If you are looking for a textured wall, select the textured split block and slump block. The split form has a rough face, and slump block has sags or slumps, lending itself to interesting dimensional effects. It is also possible to use two types of blocks in one wall to create an interesting pattern; for example, alternate a row of 8-inch blocks with 4-inch ones.

There are different ways of treating the mortared joints. A tooled joint is sort of a half-round cove or squeezed joint, where mortar is allowed to show between the joints. A raked joint produces a sharp relief; this is done by cleaning the mortar from the joint to a depth of ½ inch or less.

Decorative block (grille) is different and also very popular because each unit is a frame surrounding a grille, fretwork, or contoured design. Depending upon the pattern, the decorative screen-block wall may be very open or very closed. This has advantages

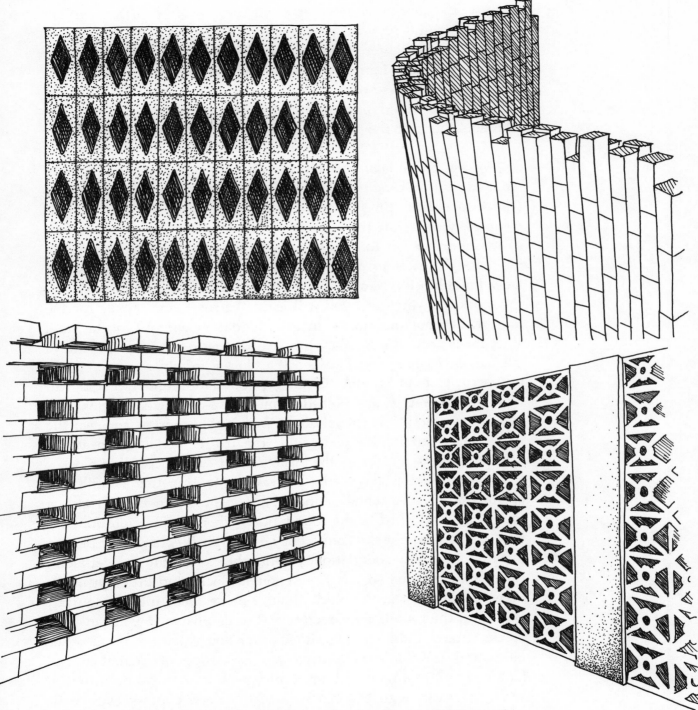

Designs of Decorative Blocks

because the design is invariably pleasing in comparison with a solid wall, and it provides air circulation and a modicum of privacy. The blocks are light weight; inexpensive; easy to clean by hosing; impervious to fire, termites, or rust; and can be laid by the average person with little difficulty. Patterns range from Mediterranean motifs to Moorish designs; most are indeed handsome and add considerable charm to the property.

Laying the block wall.   A block wall needs a substantial footing (foundation) of concrete. The foundation may be 18 or 24 inches (check local frost lines). Pour the foundation in forms; when it is completely dry, start the wall work. Use a mortar mix: 2 shovelfuls of masonry cement to about 5 shovelfuls of mortar and sand. Use just enough water to make the mix plastic so that it clings to the trowel and block without running or squeezing down when you lay the block. As you work you will learn the right consistency for the mortar. Lay out the blocks on the foundation without mortar, and shift them around until they fit. The idea is to save you having to cut blocks. Keep spaces between the blocks no wider than ½ inch, no narrower than ¼ inch. Clean the foundation and wet it down. Now mix mortar, or use a plastic cement or a pre-mixed mortar (you add only water). Now trowel on a 2-inch bed of mortar, and seat the first block. Tap it into place with the trowel handle. Repeat the process, putting mortar on the inside end of each succeeding block.

For a sturdier wall, lay the block on a footing that is still in a plastic state (consistency of mortar). The first course of blocks is then solidly attached to the foundation. When the concrete foundation has become like the consistency of mortar it is ready for blocks, but first, as in any foundation, position blocks on the ground along the side foundation so you have enough blocks and little cutting is necessary. Then seat the block about 2 inches deep into the mortar. You want the foundation concrete still to be pliable so you can level blocks. Start at the corner with a level and square-shaped corner block, and trowel mortar in strips on outside edges of the first course. Do one block at a time and tap it into position. Always be sure it is level and flush with the block beneath. Keep courses even with a mason line. (See brick section following for mortar properties.) Put down just enough mortar for one block at a time.

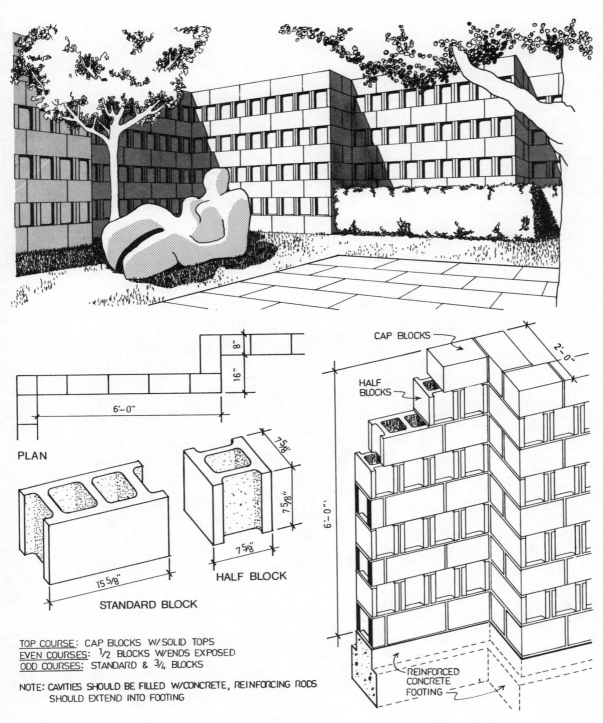

PLAN

7 5/8"

7 5/8"

7 5/8"

15 5/8"

STANDARD BLOCK

HALF BLOCK

8"

16"

6'-0"

CAP BLOCKS

HALF BLOCKS

2'-0"

6'-0"

REINFORCED CONCRETE FOOTING

TOP COURSE: CAP BLOCKS W/SOLID TOPS
EVEN COURSES: 1/2 BLOCKS W/ENDS EXPOSED
ODD COURSES: STANDARD & 3/4 BLOCKS

NOTE: CAVITIES SHOULD BE FILLED W/CONCRETE, REINFORCING RODS
SHOULD EXTEND INTO FOOTING

Concrete Block Wall

design/drawing : Adrian Martinez

① String out the block on the footing

② Spread mortar for the first few blocks

③ Place the end block solidly in the mortar

④ Butter ends of face shells of each block

⑤ Use a mason's level or straight board to check alignment

⑥ Make sure that blocks are true

⑦ Place mortar for horizontal joints along face shells of blocks already laid

Block Wall Construction

If you place a wall where there is a drainage problem, you will have to put drain tiles along the outer edge. Slope the wall about 1 inch for each 15 feet. Be sure to cover the joints with roofing paper and backfill with gravel.

For tall walls (over 5 feet), use reinforcing rods set vertically and solidly in the concrete foundation. Space them according to local building codes. Lay the first course of the wall in wet concrete, and then drive the rods through the cores. The holes for rods must match holes in blocks, so alignment is vital.

A screen-block wall (one with designs) is laid on a foundation, and then the block is installed with epoxy mortars; these mortars are extremely strong, and thus generally no reinforcing rods are necessary. The tops and sides of the blocks are covered with epoxy (from a caulking gun) and blocks are set in place. All materials can be found at local building-supply houses.

Brick. The beauty of brick cannot be denied; it is a natural material that harmonizes with most outdoor situations. Whether in a straight, L shaped, or serpentine wall, brick offers charm and stands the test of time. Furthermore, brick offers a multitude of patterns: thin, thick, colored, rectangular.

The average brick wall is 8 or more inches thick (two bricks wide) and requires steel reinforcing rods in mortar joints at frequent intervals. Very large walls will have to be reinforced about every 12 feet with a brick pier or pilaster. This type of construction requires the help of a professional mason. You can dictate the pattern to suit your tastes, but the actual building of the wall (unless you are very handy with tools) generally must be farmed out. However, for those who want to try constructing their own brick wall, you will need these tools: pointed trowel for buttering mortar; broad-bladed cold chisel; hammer, level, and carpenter's square.

Common brick must be damp to be laid; to hold the mortar you need a mortar board: a piece of wood, say, a top of an orange crate. Scoop the mortar (enough for only a few bricks) from the board with the trowel, and spread it over the top course of bricks. Put each brick in place, trim away mortar to butter the end of the next brick, and continue until more mortar is needed. Bricks should be set in perfect alignment; tap them into place gently. Build the

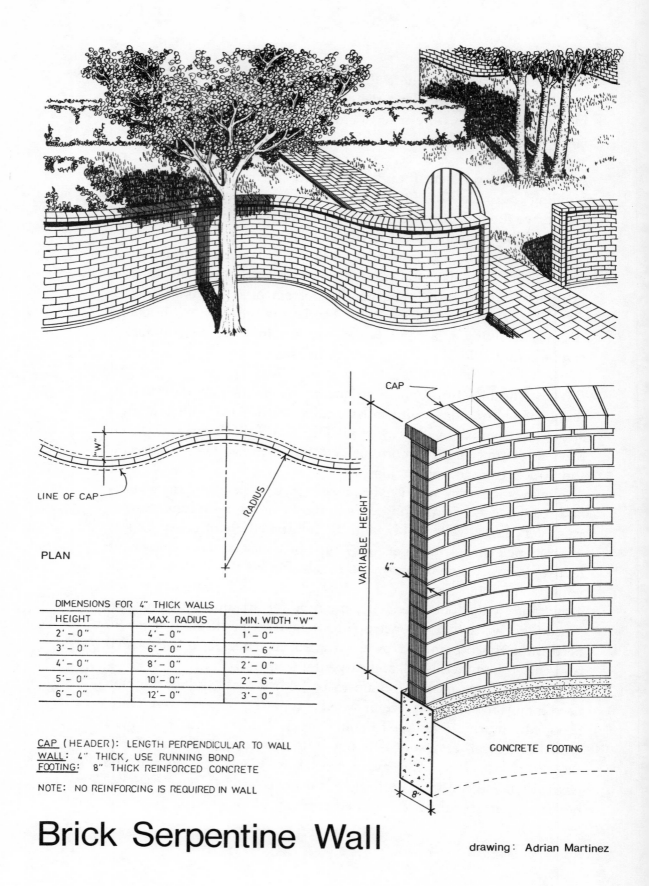

LINE OF CAP

RADIUS

PLAN

CAP

VARIABLE HEIGHT

4"

CONCRETE FOOTING

8"

DIMENSIONS FOR 4" THICK WALLS

HEIGHT	MAX. RADIUS	MIN. WIDTH "W"
2' – 0"	4' – 0"	1' – 0"
3' – 0"	6' – 0"	1' – 6"
4' – 0"	8' – 0"	2' – 0"
5' – 0"	10' – 0"	2' – 6"
6' – 0"	12' – 0"	3' – 0"

CAP (HEADER): LENGTH PERPENDICULAR TO WALL
WALL: 4" THICK, USE RUNNING BOND
FOOTING: 8" THICK REINFORCED CONCRETE

NOTE: NO REINFORCING IS REQUIRED IN WALL

Brick Serpentine Wall

drawing: Adrian Martinez

ends or corners first in steps because this will make it easier to set the next bricks in line. Be sure to use a strong guide line, that is, a nylon line to guide you in laying the bricks. Anchor the ends of the line into mortar joints. Before the mortar sets, trim away loose bits and smooth off all joints.

Brick and wood combine to make a perfectly lovely fencing in this photo; brick blends well in almost any garden setting. (*Photo courtesy Theodore Birckman, Landscape Architects*)

Old rubble brick is used for this slightly curved garden wall; it adds the necessary weight and charm to make this garden appealing. (*Photo by Matthew Barr*)

Mortar for brick laying is a mixture of cement, fine sand, and water, with some lime added for plasticity: 2 parts Portland cement, 1 part fireclay or lime, and 9 parts garden sand. Supplies are sold at hardware and lumber stores.

Stone and Poured Concrete. Stone walls are like putting jigsaw puzzles together because each stone must set into place perfectly. The skilled stoneworker can create a wall that appears as if each stone was precut before assembling. As an amateur you will have to be content with less than perfection because stone walls are difficult to build (but not impossible).

The beauty of stone walls is in their natural look and their countrified character. And there are many beautiful stones to use: Stratified rock such as limestone, shale, and sandstone are very pleasing, and granite and basalt rock are equally handsome.

Stone walls can be made of either uncut stones, known as rubble, or with cut stones, known as ashlars. Unstratified stones are difficult to cut and thus are generally laid in rubble form. I think the rubble wall is more difficult to perfect than the ashlar type be-

A masonry stone wall adds charm to this home. The handsome texture and pattern is easy to look at. (*Photo by Matthew Barr*)

cause with rubble you have to fit and juggle, while ashlars are relatively simple to put in place.

When you are working with stone be sure of your design from the start; the wall should appear natural, as you would see the stones on the ground, never upended or in an awkward position. You will have to work as you go along with the design, so an eye for aesthetics is necessary. There is no set pattern for a stone wall; it depends upon the stones used and your own personal judgment.

Like most walls, stone walls require a good foundation of concrete to avoid cracking and splitting. In cold climates the frost line is about 26 inches ((check with local building codes). Start the actual stone structure a little below the surface of the ground, and lay it directly with mortar on the concrete foundation.

Here a retaining wall is made of randomly selected stones and the effect is totally handsome. It is natural and lovely. (*Photo by Matthew Barr*)

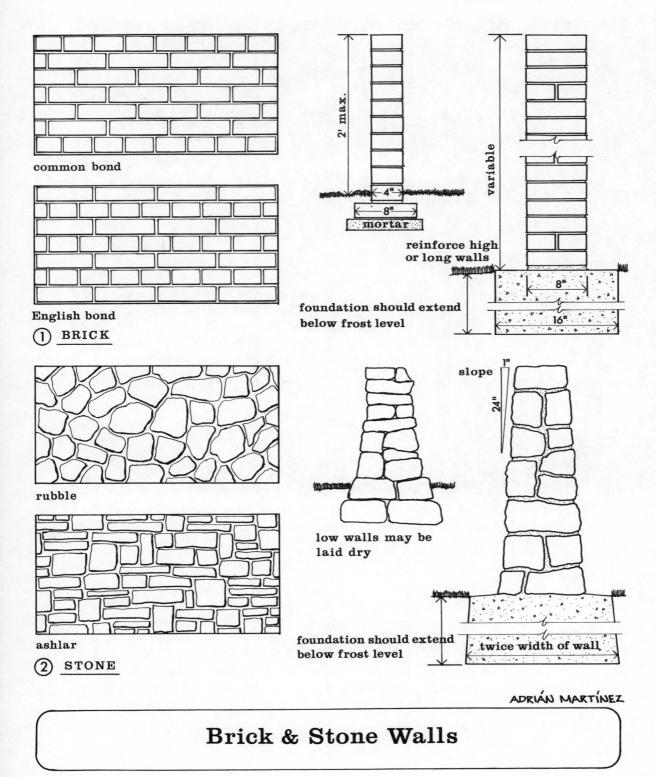

common bond

English bond

① BRICK

rubble

ashlar

② STONE

2' max.

4"

8"

mortar

reinforce high
or long walls

variable

8"

16"

foundation should extend
below frost level

low walls may be
laid dry

slope 1"

24"

foundation should extend
below frost level

twice width of wall

ADRIÁN MARTÍNEZ

Brick & Stone Walls

Concrete block is used in a simple pattern to form this retaining wall; it is straight and square and a perfect foil for the lush plantings. (*Photo by Ken Molino*)

If you decide to tackle your own stone wall (and let me warn you, it is not easy), here are some hints:

1. Keep plenty of stones ready; it is much easier to fit a stone in place when you have a choice rather than to force it in place.
2. Use plenty of mortar to fill in all joints. Where there are spaces fill in with chunks of stone and mortar over them.
3. String guide lines and keep the face of the structure flush.

Concrete walls have many advantages: A poured wall can be almost any shape, it is extremely strong, and surface texture can be in several finishes, such as textured, smooth, or embossed. But cast concrete is hardly a job for the do-it-yourselfer. Precise forms are necessary, and careful pouring of concrete is essential to create a handsome wall. This particular kind of wall building is best left for professionals.

Retaining Walls.   Retaining walls do more than hold back a hill; they can and should be decorative too. A dry stone wall installation with plants in earth "pockets" is quite effective in the garden. So are cascading plants covering the sharp edges of masonry or wooden retaining walls.

An easy dry-wall installation is placing stones against a slope; between the stones leave earth pockets. The stones should be chosen to pitch the wall back toward the thrust of the slope. Dry stone walls are not difficult to build and also offer the gardener the chance to grow small plants between the stones—a fascinating kind of gardening, very decorative for an area. Keep dry walls to a maximum of 4 feet; higher walls are apt to tumble with time if there are severe rains.

A retaining wall of over 4 feet is not easily constructed and it is best to seek professional help with these structures. Remember that if the wall is not properly engineered and built, it might collapse after the first few rainstorms. However, low walls as mentioned can be made by the average homeowner with little cost.

A main consideration of any retaining wall is that there is ample provision for water drainage. Soil absorbs a large quantity of water during a rainy season; it flows downhill below the surface. Where the water hits the wall it accumulates and collects, building up pressure, and may burst the wall.

Weep holes in the wall is the simplest way of getting rid of excess water; tile and gravel backfill will also prevent undermining of a wall. Where weep holes are used, construct a special gutter to carry off water so it doesn't ruin patio or lawn. Standard drain tiles or rounded concrete gutters can be used. All gutters should be wide enough to shovel away debris—leaves, twigs—if necessary.

Again, let me say that where the wall is over 4 feet or the slope of the hillside more than 30 percent, seek outside help.

Masonry retaining walls.   A masonry retaining wall may be brick, concrete block, or cast concrete. In any event it is better to have a series of low walls than one high one; it is less likely to lean or break under pressure. Concrete foundations and reinforcing rods will be necessary with any masonry wall.

Brick retaining walls are lovely but they are difficult to build. Even when securely mortared they do not have the holding power of a concrete wall. Reinforcing rods are necessary in brick, as are weep holes, and this is a job best left to the professional. However, for all their problems a brick wall lends old-world charm to a garden, so if it is your choice have it built but be sure it is built to stay.

Wooden retaining walls.   Redwood or cedar boards are frequently used for low retaining walls (terrace beds, too) and these are effective in appearance and function well if built properly. However, even with these resistant woods, do use a fungicide preservative on any wooden member that comes in contact with the soil. Generally 2 x 12-inch boards are run horizontally and 4 x 4-inch posts support them. Dig deep post holes (about 28 inches) and use a gravel base as for regular fence work. Place posts every 4 feet for support and you might also want to brace the wall with wooden members.

Plant vines and trailers in the earth; in time they will drape the wall in rich green.

Mixing Concrete

Concrete is a versatile plastic material composed of gravel and sand held together by cement and water. You can buy these ingredients and make your own concrete, or you can buy concrete already mixed and delivered to the job. Still another way, and an easy one, is to buy concrete in the form of a dry mix in sacks. All you have to do is add water. But for the average fence-post installation this can be very expensive, so let us first consider making your own concrete; it is not that difficult.

For foundation work and solid walls of concrete your best bet is buying ready mix delivered to the site. For laying stone, brick, or block you will generally have to mix your own (or buy it in sacks).

To estimate the amount of concrete you will need for a job, measure the length and breadth in feet and the thickness in a fraction of a foot. Multiply the three figures together to determine just how many cubic feet of concrete are needed. For example, if a foundation is 3 feet by 20 feet with a thickness of 4 inches, you would need about 20 cubic feet or about four-fifths of a cubic yard of concrete.

For mixing concrete by hand you can use a wheelbarrow, or you can rent a power or hand-operated concrete mixer. Whatever the mixing method you decide to use, the ingredients of concrete are Portland cement, fine aggregate (stones), coarse aggregate (larger

stones), and water. Portland cement is sold in sacks of 1 cubic foot. Coarse aggregate is well-ground gravel or crushed rock; fine aggregate are stones less than ¼ inch in diameter. The amount of water used per sack of cement determines the strength of concrete. Usually, less water used per sack of cement will give a better concrete.

Generally, for wall footings and foundations you should use 6 gallons of water for each sack of cement. To mix the concrete put 2 shovelfuls of sand into the wheelbarrow and add 1 shovelful of cement. Mix thoroughly, add 3 shovelfuls of gravel, and mix again. Add water from a garden hose, a little at a time, mixing as you go. Continue mixing all ingredients until they are well combined and of the desired stiffness. If you have added too much water, add some more sand, gravel, and cement. If the mixture is too thick, add more water. When using a hand or power mixer follow the same procedure.

7. Plants as Fences

Wooden fences and stone walls certainly predominate as privacy and land boundaries, but there are other ways in which to define your property. You can have natural barriers by using shrubs and trees. At first glance this may not seem as satisfactory as a man-made fence, but there are advantages to having hedges and tree barriers: You get a completely natural look, and plants can, if placed properly, screen out considerable (but not all) noise. For example, the back of my house faces a well-traveled freeway that is about a mile away. Fortunately, a thick row of cedars growing at the lower level of my property reduces traffic noise and almost screens out the view of the freeway. In a few years the cedars (now 30 feet tall) will completely screen out the road. No ordinary wood or concrete fence could accomplish this. The trees also act as wind barriers, thwarting the strong northwest winds.

Shrubs as hedges or screens are other ways to use nature to help you. They can be tall or low, evergreen or deciduous. Like trees, shrubs are a natural barrier and as such can be handsome in the garden plan.

TREES AS BARRIERS

Almost any tree can be used as a boundary to screen out a view and reduce noise pollution, although evergreens are the best choice. Trees such as cedars and junipers have dense foliage and thus are able to thwart more noise than sparsely leaved trees. To be effective, trees or shrubs should be placed close to the noise source, and where possible use taller varieties of trees. Where it is not possible to place tall trees, use shorter shrubs and grasses.

Plant the trees and shrubs as close together as possible to form a continuous dense barrier, but do not put them so close to each other that they will not have sufficient space to grow. As mentioned, evergreens are best, but some deciduous trees can be used too, if necessary.

For effective noise control with trees and shrubs, the plant belt should be as wide as possible. A single row of plants will not be as effective as, say, two rows of very tall trees with two rows of shrubs in front. The denser the belt the more noise will be reduced. And the closer the plant material is to the noise factor the better the results. In any case, trees and shrubs can and do help to reduce the noise factor but cannot be expected to create a total vacuum. There will still be some noise.

Just how much noise will seep through the natural barrier depends upon temperature, humidity, and wind velocity. Thus, each situation will dictate how much plant material to use. The natural elements refract or bend the sound rays upward or downward by changing the normal velocity, dependent upon various elevations. Temperature governs too: In summer, when cooler temperatures prevail in a tree belt, there is natural resistance to sound penetration.

Quite generally, the wide belts of trees and shrubs (50 to 75 feet) as used by highway departments to reduce noise levels will not be necessary on home grounds. The width of the barrier may be only 10 to 15 feet, but it will still afford some protection from noise and will be more effective than a board fence or concrete wall.

The drawback with natural hedges and screens is that they must have time to grow. And you must see that they grow healthily to attain the proper size and breadth to be of value to the property. When I moved into my present house I put up a redwood fence. However, knowing that the adjacent land was purchased and soon to be built on, I lined the fence at 10-foot intervals with 2 rows of evergreens. After 3 years the trees are now 20 feet high, and in another 5 years they will be tall enough to screen out the neighbors as well as reduce noise from cars (an adjacent entry road runs the length of the fence).

The Forest Service, U.S. Department of Agriculture, in cooperation with the University of Nebraska College of Agriculture, has issued a valuable booklet titled *Trees and Shrubs for Noise Abatement*. It is Research Bulletin 246 and is available from USDA free. The following list of trees and shrubs for noise abatement is taken from this booklet:

Tall Growers

Common Name	Regions of Best Adaptability
Fir	
white	Nationwide
Veitch's silver, Nikko	East
balsam	Midwest, North, Northeast
corkbark	Midwest, Southwest, Southeast
Fraser	East, Southeast
California red	West
Spanish	West Coast
Cedar	
atlas	West Coast
deodar, Cedar of Lebanon	West Coast, South, Gulf Coast
Port-Oxford cedar	West Coast, South, Southeast
Arizona cypress	Southwest, South, Southeast
Spruce	
Norway, white Serbian	Nationwide (best in North)
Oriental, blue	Nationwide (best in North)
Pine	
western white	West
ponderosa	West, Midwest
Scotch	Nationwide (best in North)
red	East, North
Austrian, eastern white	Midwest, East
Monterey	California Coast
Douglas fir	Nationwide (except South)
Giant sequoia, redwood	West Coast
Western red cedar	West
Hemlock	
eastern	East, Southeast
Carolina	East Coast, Southeast, South
western	West Coast

Medium Height

Common Name	Regions of Best Adaptability
Juniper (upright)	
eastern red cedar and varieties	East of Rock Mountains
Rocky Mountain and varieties	West of Rocky Mountains, Midwest
Chinese and varieties	Nationwide
Grecian	Nationwide
Irish	Nationwide (best in North)
Swedish	Nationwide (best in North)
Yew	
Japanese and varieties	Nationwide
English	Nationwide (best in East)
Arborvitae	
American and varieties	Nationwide (best in North, Northeast)
Oriental and varieties	South

Low Growers

Juniper	
Chinese (Pfitzer) and others	Nationwide
Mugho pine	Nationwide
Arbovitae	
American and varieties	Nationwide
Oriental and varieties	Nationwide
Yew	
Japanese and varieties	Nationwide

SHRUBS

Shrubs can be used in the same way as trees to define your property and to reduce noise pollution. Where fences will not do, or where a natural look is desired, shrubs are the answer. But when you use shrubs as hedges, remember that they will require frequent maintenance, that is, trimming and pruning. Untrimmed shrubs can become an unattractive jungle, but well-pruned plants can add a great deal to a site. Some shrubs take to trimming better than others; some do not respond to trimming and always appear shaggy. So select shrubs with care; seek compact, dense, foliaged types (see list).

1. Prunus laurocerasus (cherry laurel)
2. Prunus laurocerasus
3. Spiraea prunifolia plena (bridal wreath)

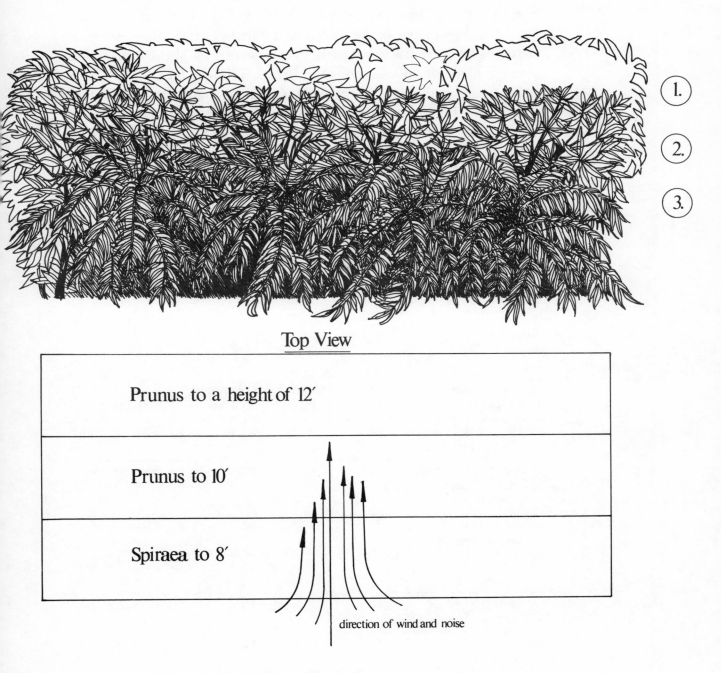

1.

2.

3.

Top View

Prunus to a height of 12′

Prunus to 10′

Spiraea to 8′

direction of wind and noise

Hedges for Screening

An attractive hedge will depend upon good proportion and placement. Stretch a string along the place to be planted, and mark a line on the ground. Make the first hole at the end of the furrow, and then decide how far apart the plants will be. Generally, privet is set 12 inches apart, barberry 12 to 16 inches, and large evergreen shrubs about 36 inches apart. Plant evergreen shrubs in fall or spring; plant deciduous ones in spring. Trim hedges wider at the base than at the top to provide sufficient light for the bottom branches. The pyramidal shape is popular, although the box shape is best for noise-abatement properties.

Shear evergreens such as yew and arborvitae either before growth starts in spring or early summer or when the new growth has had a chance to harden. Fertilize hedges sparsely or you may find yourself trimming them more than you like.

For maximum noise control make hedges wide, at least 10 feet; height will depend upon your individual needs such as privacy. Some shrubs grow tall, and others remain low; this information is included in the following list:

Shrubs

Botanical and Common Name	SE* D E	Approx. Height in Ft.	Average Temp.	Remarks
Abelia grandiflora (glossy abelia)	SE	5	—10 to —5 F.	Free flowering
Amelanchier canadensis (shablow, service berry)	D	30	—20 to —10 F.	Slow grower
Andromeda polifolia (bog rosemary)	E	1–2	—50 to —35 F.	Likes moist locations
Aucuba japonica (aucuba)	E	15	5 to 10 F.	Good for shady places
Berberis thunbergii (Japanese barberry)	D/E	7	—10 to 5 F.	Grows in any soil
Buddleia davidii (butterfly bush)	D/E	15	—10 to —5 F.	Many varieties

*SE = semievergreen   D = deciduous   E = evergreen

Shrubs and trees are used as natural barriers in this lovely pool-garden setting; the plants are massed to control noise and also to afford privacy. (*Garden designed by Eleanor B. McClure, photo by Jack Roche*)

A wall too low for the situation has natural plants to stretch its height and afford privacy and control noise. (*Photo by Matthew Barr*)

Botanical and Common Name	SE* D E	Approx. Height in Ft.	Average Temp.	Remarks
Buxus microphylla koreana (Korean boxwood)	E	6–10	—20 to —10 F.	Hardiest; foliage turns brown in winter
Callistemon citrinus (bottlebrush)	E	25	20 to 30 F.	Lovely flowers
Carissa grandiflora (Natal plum)	E	15	20 to 30 F.	Spiny, branching one
Ceanothus americanus (New Jersey tea)	E	3	—20 to —10 F.	For poor soil
C. thyrsiflorous (blue blossom)	E	30	—20 to —10 F.	Grows in sandy soil
Clethra alnifolia (summer sweet)	D	9	—35 to —20 F.	Fragrant summer bloom

*SE = semievergreen   *D = deciduous*   *E = evergreen*

Botanical and Common Name	SE* D E	Approx. Height in Ft.	Average Temp.	Remarks
Cornus mas (cornelian cherry)	D	To 18	—20 to —5 F.	Early blooming
Daphne odora (fragrant daphne)	D/E	4–6	5 to 10 F.	Fragrant
Elaeagnus angustifolia (Russian olive)	D	20	—50 to —35 F.	Fragrant flowers
E. pungens (silverberry)	D/E	12	5 to 10 F.	Vigorous grower
Erica canaliculata (heather)	E	6	20 to 30 F.	Pink, purple flower
Euonymus alata (winged euonymus)	D	9	—35 to —20 F.	Sturdy; easily grown
E. latifolius	D	20	—10 to —5 F.	Vigorous grower
Fatsia japonica (Japanese aralia)	E	15	5 to 10 F.	Handsome foliage
Forsythia ovata (early forsythia)	D	8	—20 to —10 F.	Earliest to bloom and hardiest
Fothergilla major (large fothergilla)	D	9	—10 to —5 F.	Good flowers and autumn color
Gardenia jasminoides (Cape jasmine)	E	4–6	10 to 30 F.	Fragrant
Gaultheria veitchiana (Veitch wintergreen)	E	3	5 to 10 F.	White or pink bell-shaped flowers
Hamamelis vernalis (spring witch hazel)	D	10	—10 to —5 F.	Early spring blooms
Hibiscus syriacus (shrub althaea)	D	15	—10 to —5 F.	Many varieties
Hypericum prolificum	D/SE	3	—20 to —10 F.	Very shrubby
Ilex crenata (Japanese holly)	E	20	—5 to 5 F.	Another good holly
Jasminum grandiflorum (Spanish jasmine)	SE/D	10–15	20 to 30 F.	Blooms all summer

*SE = semievergreen   D = deciduous   E = evergreen

Botanical and Common Name	SE* D E	Approx. Height in Ft.	Average Temp.	Remarks
J. officinale (common white jasmine)	SE/D	30	5 to 10 F.	Tall-growing
Juniperus communis (common juniper)	E	30	—50 to —35 F.	Many varieties
Kalmia latifolia (mountain laurel)	E	30	—20 to —10 F.	Amenable grower
Kolkwitzia amabilis (beauty bush)	D	10	—20 to —10 F.	Has many uses
Laurus nobilis (sweet bay)	E	30	—5 to 5 F.	Tough plant
Ligustrum amurense (Amur privet)	D/E	6–30	—35 to —20 F.	Small spikes of white flowers
Lonicera fragrantissima (winter honeysuckle)	D/E	3–15	—10 to —5 F.	Early fragrant flowers
L. tatarica (Tatarian honeysuckle)	D	10	—35 to —20 F.	Small pink flowers in late spring
Mahonia repens (creeping mahonia)	SE/E	1	—10 to —5 F.	Small; good ground cover
Nerium oleander (oleander)	E	15	5 to 20 F.	Popular flowering shrub
Photinia serrulata (Chinese photinia)	E	36	5 to 10 F.	Bright red berries
Pieris japonica (Japanese andromeda)	E	9	—10 to —5 F.	Splendid color
Pittsoporum tobira (Japanese pittosporum)	E	10	10 to 20 F.	Fragrant white flowers
Potentilla fruticosa (cinquefoil)	D	2–5	—50 to —35 F.	Many varieties
Raphiolepis umbellata (yeddo hawthorn)	E	6	5 to 10 F.	Sun or partial shade
Ribes sanguineum (flowering currant)	D	4–12	—10 to —5 F.	Deep red flowers March to June

*SE = semievergreen   D = deciduous   E = evergreen

Rows of shrubs and trees are the fence for this property. It retains a natural look and does the job admirably. (*Photo by Ken Molino*)

While a fence is used on this property it is the trees and shrubs that provide noise control and privacy. It is a lush, lovely look. (*Photo by Ken Molino*)

Here plants are used to soften the wire fencing as well as provide privacy and help thwart noise. As years pass the natural vegetation will give even more coverage. (*Photo by Ken Molino*)

Botanical and Common Name	SE* D E	Approx. Height in Ft.	Average Temp.	Remarks
Salix caprea (French pussy willow)	D	25	—20 to —10 F.	Vigorous grower
Skimmia japonica (Japanese skimmia)	E	4	5 to 10 F.	For shade
Spiraea prunifolia (bridal wreath spiraea)	D	9	—20 to —10 F.	Turns orange in fall
S. veitchii	D	12	—10 to —5 F.	Good background; graceful one
Syringa villosa (late lilac)	D	9	—50 to —35 F.	Dense, upright habit
Tamarix aphylla (Athel tree)	E	30–50	5 to 10 F.	Good widespread tree
Taxus canadensis (Canada yew)	E	3–6	—50 to —35 F.	Will tolerate shade
Viburnum dentatum (arrowwood)	D	15	—50 to —35 F.	Red fall color
V. lantana (wayfaring tree)	D	15	—35 to —20 F.	Grows in dry soil
V. opulus (European cranberry bush)	D	12	—35 to —20 F.	Good; many varieties
V. trilobum (cranberry bush)	D	12	—50 to —35 F.	Effective in winter
Vitex agnus-castus (chaste tree)	D	9	—5 to 10 F.	Lilac flowers
Weigela 'Bristol Snowflake'	D	7	—10 to —5 F.	Complex hybrid
Weigela middendorffiana	D	1	—20 to —10 F.	Dense, broad shrub

*SE = semievergreen   D = deciduous   E = evergreen

8. Decorative Plants for Fences and Walls

Fences as part of the total landscape design should not be barren. They need decoration to tie them into the landscape—this means lovely vines. The overall effect of vining plants on fences provides pattern, color, and contrast and contributes greatly to the setting.

Quite frankly, vines cover a multitude of sins. Even the most common fence can become handsome with proper placement of vining plants. For example, some flowering vines, such as clematis and bougainvillea, can become breathtaking sights, and foliage vines can be used with great drama to adorn fences: Dutchman's pipe (*Aristolochia durior*) and Carolina jessamine (*Gelsemium semper-virens*) are popular favorites.

Growing plants in espalier fashion against a fence is another way to bring beauty to an ordinary fence. The espaliered plant is grown in specific patterns flat against the wood in a tailored trim look; it is lovely and further allows you to grow plants where space may be limited.

If you have a rubble or stone wall consider growing rock plants in the crevices; this creates a tapestry of color and adds great beauty to the property. Finally, if you do not have time to do extensive gardening and want quick decoration for fences, sculpture and other oddments can be blended into the setting.

VINES

For quick cover and beauty vines are a boon for gardeners; they are relatively easy to grow, and there are dozens of suitable types. Some grow rampant, so selection is vital, but there are many vines

86

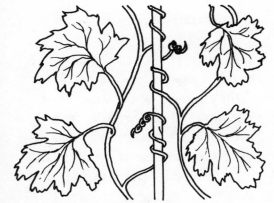

(1) COILING TENDRILS e.g., grape

(2) COILING LEAFSTALKS e.g., clematis

(3) TWINING STEMS e.g., honeysuckle, Hall's

(4) WEAVING STEMS e.g., climbing rose

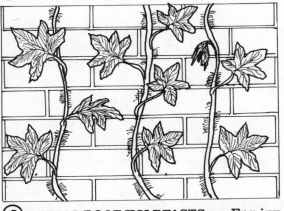

(5) AERIAL ROOT HOLDFASTS e.g., Eng. ivy

(6) ADHESIVE DISCS e.g., Boston ivy

ADRIÁN MARTÍNEZ

How Vines Cling

that with routine pruning remain neat and contribute greatly to a garden fence.

Some climbing vines like clematis, bougainvillea, and morning glory are excellent color additions to the landscape, and because they are massive and quick growing, they cover large areas in a short time. If you want a dainty, charming effect for the fence, choose sweet peas, stephanotis, or a wisteria. These are especially good for covering harsh, angular walls and fences. If you need some winter color in the garden, try euonymus, pyracantha, or bittersweet, they bear colorful winter berries, which give a dramatic contrast to gray winter skies.

Some vines climb with twining stems that need support, but others have tendrils or disks. Other vines have leaflike appendages that act as tendrils, grasping the surface they grow on. Generally, once established all vines will cover a surface with little more trouble than occasional pruning.

Plant woody vines in deep planting holes (at least 3 to 4 feet) so roots will have ample space to grow. Use good top soil and humus, and tamp the earth gently but firmly around the collar of the plant. Pat down soil to eliminate air pockets, which cause water stagnation. Water thoroughly and deeply (most vines take great quantities of water). For the first few weeks give vines close attention. See that they are growing, but once established, routine care can be given.

Put vines in the ground at the same level they were growing in the nursery can, and try not to disturb roots. When you take the plant from the container keep the root ball intact; if the roots are harmed, it will take the plant much longer to establish itself.

Once a week feed vines with a mild fertilizer solution to keep them in good health, and prune and thin at regular intervals to keep them looking handsome. Here are ideal vines for fences:

Botanical and Common Name	Min. Night Temp.	General Description	Sun or Shade	Remarks
Akebia quinata (five-leaf akebia)	—20 to —10 F.	Vigorous twiner; fragrant small flowers	Sun or partial shade	Needs support; prune in fall/early spring

Vines offer fine decoration for fences; this clematis is especially appealing for color and beauty. (*Photo by author*)

Ivy espaliers easily and is a favorite plant to grow in this manner; the effect is delicate yet handsome. (*Photo courtesy California Redwood Assoc.*)

Botanical and Common Name	Min. Night Temp.	General Description	Sun or Shade	Remarks
Allamanda cathartica	Tender	Dense w/ heavy stems, lovely tubular flowers	Sun	Prune annually in spring
Ampelopsis breviped-unculata (porcelain ampelopsis) (blueberry climber)	—20 to —10 F.	Strong grower w/ dense leaves	Sun or shade	Prune in early spring
Antigonon leptopus (coral vine)	Tender	Excellent as screen	Sun	Needs light support; prune hard after bloom
Aristolochia durior (Dutchman's pipe)	—20 to —10 F.	Big twiner w/mammoth leaves	Sun or shade	Needs sturdy support; prune in spring or summer
Clytostoma *Bignonia capreolata* (cross vine) (trumpet vine)	—5 to 5 F.	Orange flowers	Sun or shade	Thin out weak branches in spring; clings by disks
Celastrus scandens (American bittersweet)	—50 to —35 F.	Light green leaves, red berries	Sun or shade	Prune in early spring before growth starts
Clematis armandi (evergreen clematis)	5 to 10 F.	Lovely flowers and foliage; many colors	Sun	Needs support; prune lightly after bloom
Doxantha unguis-cati	10 to 20 F.	Dark green leaves, yellow blooms	Sun	Needs no support; prune hard after bloom
Euonymus fortunei (wintercreeper)	—35 to —20 F.	Shiny leathery leaves; orange berries in fall	Sun or shade	Needs support; prune in early spring

Morning glory, clematis, and bamboo climb this wooden fence softening the scene. (*Photo by Matthew Barr*)

Botanical and Common Name	Min. Night Temp.	General Description	Sun or Shade	Remarks
Fatshedera lizei	20 to 30 F.	Grown for handsome foliage	Shade	No pruning needed
Ficus pumila (repens) (creeping fig)	20 to 30 F.	Small heart-shaped leaves	Partial shade	Thin plant in late fall or early spring
Gelsemium sempervirens (Carolina jessamine)	Tender	Fragrant yellow flowers	Sun or partial shade	Needs support; thin plant immediately after bloom
Hedera helix (English ivy)	—10 to —5 F.	Scalloped neat leaves; many varieties	Shade	Prune and thin in early spring
Hydrangea petiolaris (climbing hydrangea)	—20 to —10 F.	Heads of snowy flowers	Sun or partial shade	Thin and prune in winter or early spring
Ipomoea purpurea (Convolvulus) (morning glory)	Tender	White, blue, purple, and pink flowers	Sun	Bloom until frost
Jasminum nudiflorum	—10 to —5 F.	Yellow flowers	Sun or shade	Needs strong support; thin and shape annually after bloom
J. officinale (white jasmine)	5 to 10 F.	Showy dark green leaves and white flowers	Sun or shade	Provide strong support; thin and shape after bloom
Kadsura japonica (scarlet kadsura)	5 to 10 F.	Bright red berries in fall	Sun	Needs support; prune annually in early spring
Lonicera caprifolium (sweet honeysuckle)	—19 to —5 F.	White or yellow trumpet flowers	Sun	Prune in fall or spring

Botanical and Common Name	Min. Night Temp.		General Description	Sun or Shade	Remarks
L. hildebrandiana (Burmese honeysuckle)	20 to	30 F.	Shiny dark green leaves	Sun or partial shade	Needs support; prune in late fall
L. japonica 'Halliana' (Hall's honeysuckle)	—20 to	—10 F.	Deep green leaves, bronze in fall	Sun or shade	Provide support; prune annually in fall and spring
Mandevilla suaveolens (Chilean jasmine)	20 to	30 F.	Heart-shaped leaves and flowers	Sun	Trim and cut back lightly in fall; remove seed pods as they form
Parthenocissus quinquefolia (Virginia creeper)	—35 to	—20 F.	Scarlet leaves in fall	Sun or shade	Prune in early spring
Passiflora caerulea (passion flower)	5 to	10 F.	Spectacular flowers	Sun	Needs support; prune hard annually in fall or early spring
Phaseolus coccineus (scarlet runner bean)	Tender		Bright red flowers	Sun	Renew each spring
Plumbago capensis (plumbago)	20 to	30 F.	Blue flowers	Sun	Prune somewhat in spring
Pueraria thunbergiana (Kudzo vine)	—5 to	5 F.	Purple flowers	Sun or partial shade	Provide sturdy support; cut back hard annually in fall
Rosa (rambler rose)	—10 to	—5 F.	Many varieties	Sun	Needs support; prune out dead wood, shorten long

Here a camellia is used in espalier fashion to decorate a fence and break the bare expanse of wood. (*Photo by Phil Palmer*)

Botanical and Common Name	Min. Night Temp.	General Description	Sun or Shade	Remarks
Rosa (*continued*)				shoots, and cut laterals back to 2 nodes in spring or early summer after bloom
Smilax rotundifolia (horse brier)	—20 to —10 F.	Good green foliage	Sun or shade	Prune hard annual any time; needs no support
Trachelospermum jasminoides (star jasmine)	20 to 30 F.	Dark green leaves and small white flowers	Partial shade	Provide heavy support; prune very lightly in fall
Vitis coignetiae (glory grape)	—10 to 5 F.	Colorful autumn leaves	Sun or partial shade	Needs sturdy support; prune annually in fall or spring
Wisteria floribunda (Japanese wisteria)	—20 to —10 F.	Violet-blue flowers	Sun	Provide support and prune annually once mature to shorten long branches after bloom or in winter; pinch back branches first year

Espalier Plants

Espaliered plants are graceful and charming, take a minimum of space, and to establish a particular character—formal, informal—to a garden they cannot be beat. But such things of beauty do not come easy: Espaliered plants need training and trimming to a desired shape. Generally the plant is tied to a trellis or fence with vine clamps or

Camellias in a triangular espalier make a handsome pattern on a horizontal board fence. (*Photo by Phil Palmer*)

staples. It is much easier to buy an espalier already started than to train one yourself.

In addition to making a bare wall or fence a thing of beauty, espaliers let you use certain trees and shrubs where space would not permit them to develop naturally. It is gardening with an artist's eye because the texture of the stems, the variation of leaf color and pattern, and the total design must be given careful consideration. It is somewhat like painting a picture on a fence with leaves and flowers.

There are numerous espalier patterns you can use for a fence, but for simplicity we can classify them as

> *Double horizontal cordon*: A center shoot about 20 inches high, with two horizontal branches in each direction.
> *Vertical U shape*: A vertical stem on each side of a central trunk. (Double and triple U shapes are also seen.)
> *Palmette verrier*: A handsome candelabra pattern (my favorite).
> *Palmette oblique*: Branches trained to a fan shape.
> *Horizontal T*: A multiple horizontal cordon, with several horizontals on each side of a vertical trunk.
> *Belgian espalier*: A diamond pattern.
> *Arcure*: A series of connecting arcs.

In each case the design chosen will impart a different character to the fence and add dimension and grace to the garden.

Select suitable plants for espaliering. Some, like morning glories, grow too rapidly, and those that have large leaves are not good choices. Dwarf fruit trees are especially suitable, and camellias and pyracantha are often seen. Magnolias and laurel are other good choices.

You can grow an espalier in the ground or in containers placed close to the fence. The plants will need a well-drained rich soil. Some want sun, but several do fine in the shade of a north or west exposure. Do not fertilize espaliers with a heavy hand; too much feeding encourges rampant growth and makes it almost impossible to keep the plants trained to the desired shape.

For supporting devices use redwood strips, wire, or bamboo as a framework. For a masonry wall, rawl plugs may be placed in the mortared joints and screw eyes inserted. Branches of plants can be held in place with raffia or soft cotton twine.

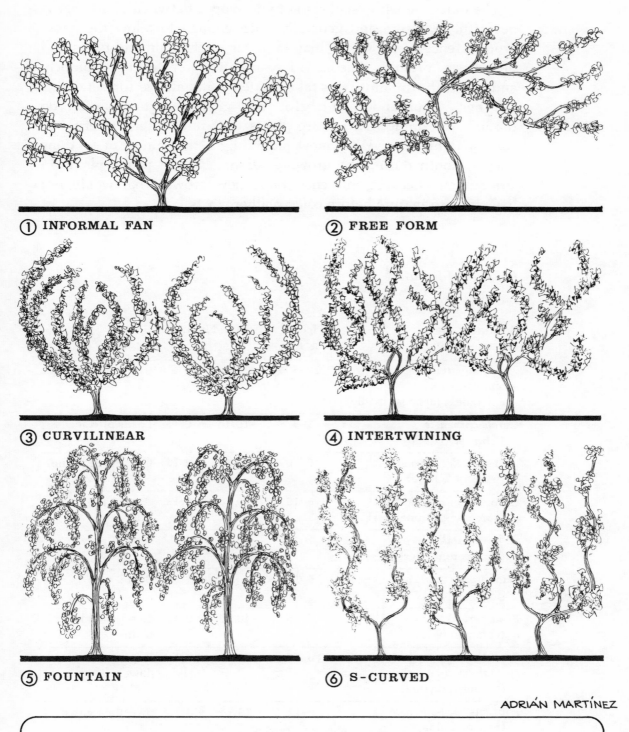

① INFORMAL FAN

② FREE FORM

③ CURVILINEAR

④ INTERTWINING

⑤ FOUNTAIN

⑥ S-CURVED

ADRIÁN MARTÍNEZ

Informal Espaliers

The objective with espaliers is to develop a flattened plant that is beautiful in design and generally open enough to allow the background fence to show. To maintain this effect, thin the twigs and branches as often as necessary. Pay attention to every twig, branch, and leaf with trimming; this takes patience and an eye for detail.

When a plant is dormant before new growth starts in spring, do the heavy pruning. On mature plants wait until after flowering to start shaping them. With most plants, light trimming can be done once a month during the growing season. Do not prune plants in late summer because this encourages new growth that would not have time to mature before cold weather starts.

Espaliers for Sun

Botanical and Common Name	Approx. Height in Ft.	Min. Night Temp.	Remarks
Acer palmatum atropurpureum (bloodleaf Japanese maple)	10–30	—10 to 0 F.	Colorful in autumn
Cercis chinensis (Chinese redbud)	3–8	—10 to 0 F.	Loads of color
Chaenomeles sinensis (Chinese quince)	10–30	—10 to 0 F.	Colorful in autumn
Cotoneaster divaricata (spreading cotoneaster)	6–15	—20 to —10 F.	Attractive summer foliage
C. horizontalis (rock cotoneaster)	1–4	—10 to 0 F.	Robust grower
Eriobotyra japonica (loquat)	6–12	Tender	Bold leaves
Ficus carica (common fig)	6–15	—10 to 0 F.	Good, bold leaf plant
Forsythia intermedia spectabilis (border forsythia)	6–15	—20 to —10 F.	Bright colors, big flowers
Hibiscus rosa-sinensis (rose of China)	6–12	—10 to 0 F.	Sweetly scented

Botanical and Common Name	Approx. Height in Ft.	Min. Night Temp.	Remarks
Jasminum nudiflorum (winter jasmine)	6–12	—10 to 0 F.	Sweetly scented
Juniperus chinensis sargenti (Sargent juniper)	1–6	—30 to —20 F.	Attractive
Magnolia grandiflora (southern magnolia)	10–30	0 to 10 F.	Large flowers
M. stellata (star magnolia)	6–15	—10 to —5 F.	Handsome white flowers
Malus astrosanguinea (carmine crab apple)	10–30	—30 to —20 F.	Early spring bloom
Pinus aristata (bristlecone pine)	1–4	—40 to —30 F.	Good in city
Prunus subhirtella pendula (Japanese weeping cherry)	10–30	—10 to 0 F.	Lovely shape
Taxus cuspidata (Japanese yew)	3–8	—20 to —10 F.	Handsome summer foliage
Viburnum prunifolium (black haw virburnum)	10–30	—40 to —30 F.	Spring bloom
V. sieboldi (siebold viburnum)	10–30	—20 to —10 F.	Ornamental fruit

Espaliers for Shade

Botanical and Common Name	Approx. Height in Ft.	Min. Night Temp.	Remarks
Camellia japonica (Japanese camellia)	10–30	0 to 10 F.	Many varieties
Carissa grandiflora (natal plum)	6–15	Tender	Bold green leaves
Chaenomeles speciosa (flowering quince)	6–12	—20 to —10 F.	Very colorful

Botanical and Common Name	Approx. Height in Ft.	Min. Night Temp.	Remarks
Cornus mas (cornelian cherry)	10–30	—20 to —10 F.	Amenable plant
Euonymus alatus (winged euonymus)	6–15	—40 to —30 F.	Good in city
Ilex crenata (Japanese holly)	10–30	—10 to 0 F.	Handsome
Pyracantha coccinea lalandi (firethorn)	6–15	—20 to —10 F.	Colorful berries
Stewartia koreana (Korean stewartia)	10–30	—10 to 0 F.	Versatile; for many areas
Taxus baccata repandens (spreading English yew)	3–8	—20 to —10 F.	Bold, branching
Viburnum plicatum	6–15	—10 to 0 F.	Versatile; for many areas

PLANTS FOR ROCK WALLS

The stone wall is more than just a barrier because it offers the gardener a chance to grow the choice rock plants. More beautiful examples of nature are hard to find, and with flowers on the wall you can attain a three-dimensional effect.

If your wall faces south or southwest, you have an ideal location for rock plants. Most rock garden plants need good sun and during hot summer months will require frequent waterings because moisture is the key to success. In long hot summers the plants need coolness because when exposed to wind and sun they dry out quickly. Some species can tolerate drought, but there is a better harvest of flowers if ample moisture is supplied. Put plants in place in fall or very early spring. In winter some plants can go without protection against dampness and the ill effects of freezing and thawing. Mulch the plant to conserve moisture and to keep the soil cool. Plants that form heavy mats of foliage need no protection, and species that are deciduous can withstand water, but plants that have rosettes of leaves need mulching.

The following list includes specific rock plants as well as some other plants that, although not normally grown as rock plants, thrive in such a situation in my garden walls:

Plants for Rock Walls
Achillea tomentosa (yarrow)
Ajuga repens (bugleseed)
Alyssum saxatile (goldentuft)
Aquilegia vulgaris (columbine)
Campanula carpatica (bellflower)
Dianthus deltoides (maiden pink)
Geranium grandiflorum (cranesbill geranium)
Gypsophila repens (creeping gypsophila)
Iberis sempervirens (candytuft)
Iris pumila (dwarf bearded iris)
Linum perenne (flax)
Myosotis scorpiodes (forget-me-not)
Phlox sublata (moss pink)
Primula polyantha (primrose)
Sedum album (stonecrop)
Sempervivum (many)
Veronica incana (speedwell)
Viola cornuta (viola)

OTHER FENCE DECORATIONS

Like a picture on a wall, sculpture can be used to add color and drama to fences. The piece can be suspended on a nail or placed in a suitable niche in the fence where it will break the monotony of a wood expanse and furnish a focal point. Of course any sculpture you use should be impervious to weather, so select pieces carefully. Bronze, lead, marble, or redwood are suitable materials and are at home outdoors.

With sculpture, consider scale. The piece cannot be too large nor should it be so small as to appear insignificant; rather, it must seem to belong.

Garden sculpture and ornaments will lend old-world charm to a setting and can be handsome additions on or near fences.

9. Gates

Gates, like fences, need planning and designing because they too are a component of the total landscape plan. Indeed, many times gates can impart a definite mood, formal or informal, to a property.

The choice of a gate will depend upon the design of the fence. However, the gate may be of a different material and a different design. Many times it is wise to make the gate design slightly different for visual contrast. The position of the gate is important too; generally it is placed in close proximity to the house entrance, but this should not be mandatory. And do not forget that utility gates somewhere else on the property are wise choices so that deliveries can be made to the home.

Gate Facts

No matter where the entrance gate is, a definite frame or border—pilasters on each side, or horizontal members, perhaps larger or higher than the fence—is aesthetically pleasing and sets the gate apart while still including it in the fence. The most important factor is that it tells the guests immediately where the gate is. Just how much security you want and the height of the fence will determine the size of the gate. Generally we think of a gate singly, but gates may also be in pairs, with great effectiveness. Pairs of gates immediately signify the entrance to the house, and are quite handsome where there are long expanses of fence.

The gate or gates will of course get more wear and tear than the fence, so it must be built solidly and attached to the fence with heavy-duty bolts and hardware. Hanging the gate so it is straight and plumb

Wooden Gates

Gates made with random pieces of wood afford lovely texture and dimension, a perfect foil for the stone pillars. (*Photo by Matthew Barr*)

will determine whether it opens or closes properly. The average do-it-yourselfer, even with the best intentions, sometimes forgets that in wet weather gates will swell. I know this only too well because it is the mistake I made in building my own lattice gates. If possible, have

An antique wooden gate is the focal point of this patio entrance. (*Photo by Joyce R. Wilson*)

a good carpenter help you with gate construction; there is more to it than meets the eye.

BUILDING THE GATE

As mentioned, the gate may be of many different patterns and have detailing, but all gates have the same principles of construction in

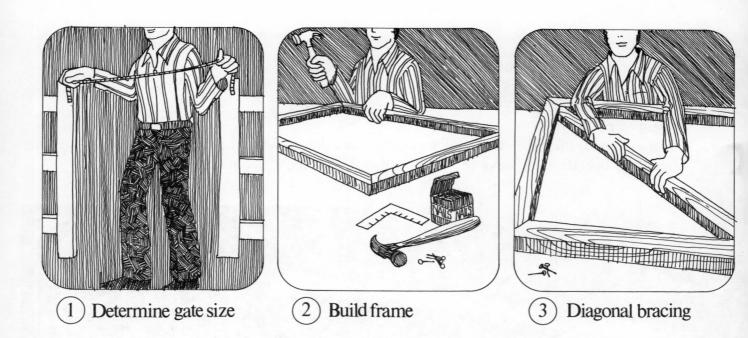

① Determine gate size ② Build frame ③ Diagonal bracing

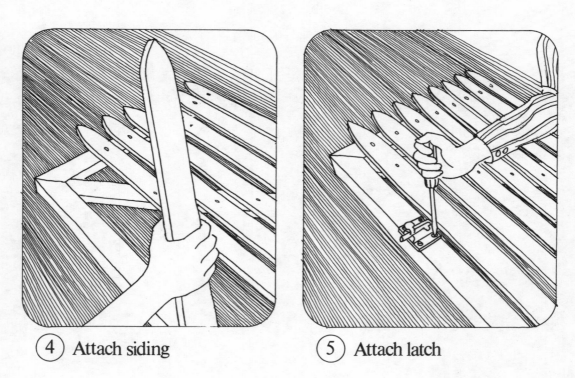

④ Attach siding ⑤ Attach latch

How to Build a Gate

common. Here are some general rules to follow when building your gate.

First get the size; measure the space between the gate posts or pilasters at both the top and bottom. It is imperative that this be

These beautiful wooden gates are handsomely designed and belong perfectly in the setting of brick and plants. (*Photo by Jack Roche*)

square or you will be heading into trouble. If the posts are not square, correct them. Plan the frame width 1 inch less than the opening. For a 48-inch opening the width of the frame should be 47 inches to allow for swing and hinge space. Now, working on a flat surface, nail and screw together the frame of the gate. Be sure to keep the frame at right angles with a square. Brace the gate with a 2 x 4 or suitable

lumber. Saw it to fit, and nail the brace at both ends through the horizontal and vertical rails. The last step is to nail in place the vertical members, starting at the hinge side of the frame.

Now that the gate is completed you will have to put hinges in place. Once again let me mention that you should use heavy-duty hinges—nothing flimsy here. Drill holes on posts and gate frame for the hinges, and screw them in place securely. Fitting the gate to the opening is done by having someone hold it in place for you while you determine if it swings freely and without sagging. Finish by putting latches on the gate.

HINGES AND LATCHES

Hinges and latches determine whether the gate stays in place a year or a day. Use overly strong hinges. Be sure screws are long enough to really anchor the hinges securely. Use four hinges on all gates over 5 feet in height. Buy weather-resistant hinges: zinc, cadmium, or the popular galvanized kinds so rusting does not stain the gate. There are various kinds of hinges: the butt, heavy T (which is quite good), and strap hinges, and of course, specially designed hardware if you want the unique.

As there are many kinds of hinges, there are also many different latches, so think before choosing. Years ago I always thought a latch was a latch and that was that. But now, after a few of my gates were wrecked by storms (or would continually blow open), I realize the value of a good latch. Ring latches are quite good and keep gates secure but I have found that the thumb latch can come loose in time, causing gates to sag. There are also hasp, bolt, and bolt-and strap latches.

Many times, the gate is the finishing touch to the total fence and landscape plan and while it may seem minor it does deserve your consideration. We all want the total setting to be handsome and that includes a proper gate.